To Shena

Thank you for
your support through
our journey

Love and
  Best Wishes
    Susan ✗ 12/11/19

Radical Home Education

Discover Home Education through the true accounts of five families

Susan J Walklate

First printing: 2019

ISBN-13: 978-0-9956849-1-1

Published by Butterfly House Publishing

British Cataloguing Publication Data:
A catalogue record of this book is available from The British Library.

I dedicate this book to my son

Simon Thorley Davies

who gives me unconditional love and has supported me
throughout our journey together.

Also to my father

Ronald Phillip Walklate

who was always so supportive in all my life choices.

I miss him every day.

'Begin at the beginning ...and go on till you
come to the end:
then stop.'

~ Lewis Carroll

'Education is not preparing for life:
education is life itself.'

~ John Dewey

Contents

Foreword

I have nothing but respect for teachers. Anyone putting themselves through years of training so they can pursue a career in helping children to realise their full potential deserves respect. However, it still comes as a shock to many teachers just how demanding their role can be. The truth is that despite all the training, you are never fully prepared for what the classroom, students, management, school governing bodies and government throw at you on a daily basis. The effort to prove you are doing your job properly involves jumping through so many hoops it can be easy to lose sight of the key task – getting the children to engage, learn and develop.

School is considered by most people to be a necessary part of life, where the young are taught their place in society and in the world. While there is much to be said for having good Ofsted scores and benchmark information about exam results, every child is unique and should be judged as a person rather than a statistic. When children are being taught how to pass specific exams, rather than how to develop their own ways of tackling and solving problems, it comes as no surprise that many who leave school with good results are not equipped to deal with life in the real world.

Unfortunately, the system of standardised assessment

used places some children at a disadvantage right from the start. Gifted musicians who cannot do maths 'fail'. Talented athletes who struggle with reading and writing 'fail'. Even the social aspect of schooling, learning how to deal with a variety of people in a myriad of situations on a daily basis, disadvantages the shy and socially awkward children who are often victimised or bullied because they are 'different' from the popular, confident ones. Spotting these problems is hard, and addressing them near impossible, thanks to the constraints of overwork, underfunding and lack of resources.

Susan took the bold step to remove Simon from school and embark on the adventure of Home Education, feeling that it was in the best interests of both his academic and emotional needs. While not following the national curriculum, she ensured that his upbringing and education brought him into contact with a wealth of information and diversity of life experiences that cannot be had in a classroom. This is their story...

Julia Tucknott
Former College Lecturer

'There is nothing in a caterpillar that tells you it's going to be a butterfly.'

~ Buckminster Fuller

'Education is what remains after one has forgotten everything he learned in school.'

~ Albert Einstein

'It takes courage to grow up
and become who you really are.'

~ E.E. Cummings

'The only impossible journey is the one you
never begin.'

~ Tony Robbins

Preface

Having a child changes your life completely. Suddenly, there's an infant who's totally dependent on you; who is the centre of your world.

I was in my mid-thirties when I had Simon. I was a self-employed freelance riding instructor and I ran a livery yard. During my pregnancy I became less able to do the physical work there and became more and more reliant on others to look after the horses. But I still went to work, and after Simon was born I took him to the yard with me and he spent his time in the tack room or in a travel cot out in the yard itself.

Luckily, he was a contented baby and a happy child, and when he started walking, he would follow me around with a wooden wheelbarrow that my father made for him, or play in the sand in the schooling area. He had complete freedom around the yard and with the horses. He seemed to be intuitively respectful of them and they in turn were remarkably careful and gentle around him.

I loved having him close to me, but many days I felt totally drained as I struggled to look after, and keep up with, this cheerful, inquisitive, fast developing small person and run the business at the same time. Often it was the business that suffered.

Looking back, I was so fortunate to have some help and support from Simon's grandparents, especially *my* parents. They all lived nearby, which was a blessing, and although Simon's father worked away during the week and sometimes for longer periods, all in all it was a happy time and Simon was a well-loved, supported and thriving child who felt safe, secure and happy to be with me.

Fast forward…

How could I possibly have known that in just a few short years it would be a very different story? And that by the time Simon was just nine years old he would become so introverted, quiet and stressed that I would hardly recognise him?

How could I have been prepared myself for his tummy aches while waiting for the school bus, or having to write letters and make frequent visits to the school to discuss what was going on for Simon there?

This was *not* my Simon.

And how could I have even begun to guess that all of this would result in a chain of events that would lead us to the decision to remove Simon from the school system he hated so much, and begin on our own daunting journey of Home Education for him?

It was quite a decision and it was quite a journey and I'll tell you more about it in Chapter 1. I'll tell you what ultimately led us to that decision, our questions, our fears and how we overcame them, the roller-coaster of highs and lows, where we got stuck and how we broke through. I'll introduce you to the people we met along the way, the resources we discovered, and what we learned from the journey, because these are, in part, what this book is all about.

But for now, fast forward again with me. Simon is now 27 years old and runs his own gardening and landscaping business. He is balanced, well-adjusted, intelligent, kind, thoughtful, ambitious, caring and a contributing member of society.

But even more than that – he is Simon: his own person, and the well-rounded and happy adult I hoped for all those years ago.

So, why did I write this book and what does it cover?

Simon's life to date is no ordinary story compared to most people's. For those who sailed through school, you may not even have noticed the children who were suddenly no longer there. You may have been unaware that they were now following a different path of education, one better suited to their needs.

Over the years, I have heard these children referred to as the *'Invisible Children'*, and Simon and I have experienced first-hand (as have many home educated families) the perception of Home Education as being the 'drop-out' choice.

However, viewed alongside the other families we shared

our journey with, Simon's story is normal. And these children – and the well-adjusted, fully-functioning young adults and contributing members of society they have become – are far from invisible.

Recently, and more than ever before, I found I wanted everyone to know that, so I decided to share their stories and celebrate all that they – that we – have achieved. I decided it was time to tell the stories of the now grown-up children who were successfully home educated. How their lives began, how their formative years progressed, and where they are now.

Starting with our story, the chapters in **Section 1: Five families joined together through Home Education** follow the lives of five home educating families and how we all came together as a cohesive group. Each of us came to Home Education from a different direction but we walked, and still walk, the path together.

Our stories are special, but not totally unique, and may resonate with many parents who are struggling with the balance of their own child's life, education and emotional wellbeing.

In **Section 2: Insight into Home Education** (Chapters 6 through 9), I'll gives you an insight into what we did and where we did it, and talk you through all the common concerns and questions we all had at the start of our journeys and those that came up along the way.

Many of them are the same questions and concerns we hear from parents today who are just embarking on this route. Questions like *Is it legal to take your child out of school? Do I have to follow the national curriculum? How will they socialise if they're not in a classroom with other children? Can I afford it? I'm not a teacher!* and so on…

Section 2 explores what we discovered, what we learnt along the way and what we created ourselves to overcome obstacles.

If school and the schooling system is failing your child, then recreating 'school' at home is not going to be the best solution. Something more radical is called for and these chapters will offer you a guide into how to do that in the most effective and enjoyable way possible.

We will also look at different learning styles and intelligences to help you better understand the best way to approach helping your child to learn in a way that works for them and will motivate them once again to embrace the joy of learning, which is their natural state.

Ultimately, a life incorporating Home Education is about giving your children choices. The choice to make decisions about their own lives. The choice of what and how they want to learn and live. It gives them the chance to flourish into functional, happy, well-rounded adults who are able play their role in society.

Who is this book for?

It's for you if you recognise yourself and your family's situation in the brief experience of ours that I just shared with you. If you're experiencing a change in your child's behaviour because of school – if your happy, learning, growing toddler has become unhappy, insecure, 'backward', angry or anything else out of character and you feel like you are losing your child – then maybe the school system is failing them as I believe it was failing Simon. I hope you might find in these pages the courage and confidence you need to take your own first steps into Home Education.

It's for you if you've already made that decision and you're looking for inspiration, reassurance and practical tips from people who have been there, done it, and got the T-shirt.

It's for you if you are a family member, grandparent or good friend of a family who has chosen to home educate, so you can better understand the choice they've made and learn how you can support their decision and help them to make things work for the good of everyone involved.

It's for you if you are a teacher or are in some way connected to mainstream education. I hope these stories will inspire you to recognise that one size does not fit all, to look for the signs that school might, in fact, be crippling a child, and to consider Home Education as a viable, perhaps infinitely preferable solution for that particular individual rather than trying to apply more and more of what's not working.

And it's for you if you're a policy or news maker, because I truly hope that by reading the stories of these families and their children and the vibrant, resilient, well-rounded, happy and contributing young people they have become, you will represent and treat Home Education and the families who choose it in the light they deserve.

The media has the power to shape all our perceptions

about education, about what we value as a society, about ourselves.

Looking back, two very different Channel 4 documentaries about Home Education, 18 years apart, were fundamental to our family's choices. The first one started this journey, and the more recent one prompted this book.

Are you ready for the roller coaster?

Then let's go....

Introduction

Section 7 of the 1996 Education Act

"The parent of every child of compulsory school age shall cause him to receive efficient full-time education suitable;

a) to his age, ability and aptitude, and

b) to any special educational needs he may have,

either by regular attendance at school or otherwise."

Home Education comes under the "…or otherwise" part of this law.

By choosing Home Education, I was fulfilling my parental obligation to provide my child with an appropriate education with regard to the law.

Section 1

Five families joined together through Home Education

'Every student can learn,
just not the same day, or the same way.'

~ George Evans

'It does not matter how slowly you go
as long as you do not stop.'

~ Confucius

Chapter 1
Simon's Story

I first came across Home Education in the mid-1980s, when my ponies lived in a field adjacent to an old farmhouse in North Swindon. This is where I met some home educated children, who lived in the farmhouse there. I would chat with the children as they rode my ponies along the bridle path nearby. They were very chatty and friendly, and quite grown up and sociable for their years. They told me about not going to school and I think I may have quizzed them a bit about what they knew.

I remember thinking, "What an odd thing to do," because I, like most of society, believed that all children went to school; it was the natural course of events. I remembered my own school experience as a reasonably positive time, and I suggested to one of the children that it would be good fun for her to go to school. She decided to try it, but after two weeks she gave it up. "The other children were mean to me," she said. I was saddened that she had a bad experience, but I didn't think about it again until nearly 20 years later when I would be considering Home

Education as the best option for my son, who was having problems at school.

Simon's life before Home Education

Simon was a contented child and he was happy to be with other people. He felt secure with me and would settle well with the people I chose to leave him with, especially my parents, who he called Nanny and Grampy Ducks, because they took him to Lydiard Park to feed the ducks.

When he was nearly two years old, he spent four days with some friends, who took him to visit his father when he was working near Newcastle Upon Tyne. Simon was happy to be with them and his father and away from me. In contrast, four years later, when we all went to Disney, Florida, with the same friends, Simon had become clingy, introverted and solemn, and insisted on being with me at all times. "What's going on? This is not like Simon!" our friends said, which brought his behaviour to my attention; over time you don't always notice the little changes until someone else sees the big differences. Why was he like this? What had changed? The only difference I could see was that he was now attending school full time. Was this the problem?

At about the same time we went to Florida, Simon had been put on the special needs register at school, because he wasn't learning to read and write as quickly as they thought he should. He found the content of the reading scheme books boring and thought reading was of no relevance to him. He had a bookshelf full of books in his bedroom at home but showed very little interest in them. He also showed little interest in wielding a pencil or paint brush; he much preferred to be outside with the animals. His gross motor skills were still developing and he was not ready to sit down and tune his fine motor skills, so writing was a struggle. In addition, his writing speed was too slow for him to keep up with the thoughts whizzing through his brain. He was aware he couldn't form his letters very well, it took a long time to write anything and he actually disliked having to write at all because his hand hurt. We only pieced these things together when he was older and able to express himself.

The other challenge for Simon was that he could not ride a two-wheeler bicycle to save his life and, likewise, was not very well balanced on his pony, even though he had been riding since before he could walk. He pedalled backwards but could not do it forwards and he could not steer the handlebars, however hard he tried; I tried to help him by holding up the bike.

My sister introduced me to Edu-K (Educational Kinesiology®), or Brain Gym (see more about this in Chapter 9). Brain Gym is a movement therapy designed to wake up the brain and stimulate brain function. Its focus is on improving learning and mental organisation.

My sister had found it very effective for her younger daughter, who was struggling with her GCSEs.

I took Simon along to a practitioner in Stroud, who did what they do … things like cross crawls, lazy eights, double doodles, etcetera.

The following week the class teacher took me to one side and said: "What has happened to Simon? He is doing so much better this week." That week he got on his two-wheeler bicycle and rode it forward in a straight line, having not been on it since struggling so hard with it. His balance and control with his bicycle and his pony had significantly improved. He still struggled with and avoided using a pencil whenever he could, but this tied in with him not being able to write as quickly as his thoughts materialised.

Simon liked his teacher in Year 2. She was aware that he was struggling and being picked on a bit by the other children, though she pointed out to me that one of the children on his table, who kept telling him to hurry up, was also slow in her work.

This teacher suggested that Simon was assessed by the Special Education Needs Coordinator (SENCO) from the County Education Department. From this assessment it was deemed that it wasn't that Simon couldn't do it, he just couldn't see the point. He has subsequently expressed to me that he found school boring and it did not inspire him. It was more fun to be out playing and running around.

In Year 3 it became evident that things were getting worse for Simon. He now caught the school bus from outside our house to the Upper School in the next village. We would stand there waiting for the bus and Simon would say that his tummy hurt. It was a genuine emotional pain that he later described as a tight knot with a sharp knife twisting in the middle of his tummy. Occasionally I would let him stay home, but if he went to school this pain would last until morning break when he was able to go out and release some of the tension.

This pain re-emerged eight years later when he stood at the bus stop waiting for the bus to take him to college for his first day. (More about that later.)

Year 3 was hard for Simon, as the class teacher picked on him. He had got to the stage of not understanding what he was supposed to be doing; he was too scared to ask her, and she would then shout at him because she thought he was being lazy. She would also blame him for things that other children had done, which he felt was unfair. This set him up to be the scapegoat for both the class teacher and the other children.

Things seemed to have settled down when Simon moved out of her class, so it was a surprise to me when, in the summer term of Year 4, he refused to go to school for 10 days. I don't know what provoked this. He returned to school because he didn't think he had a choice other than to just make the best of it and later, in Year 5, he got on with being there as the teacher was okay.

Electing to enrol my child with the local school, I had assumed that they would look after him and have his best interests at heart. Sadly, this is not necessarily the truth and I began to realise that I needed to be more proactive in supporting Simon at school. Though he had been put on the special needs register and had a plan of action it became apparent that nothing was being done about this. When he was eight, I requested a copy of each of his action plans and received them, though there was resistance from the school. I asked for him to be reassessed by the SENCO and for him to be statemented to level 4, as he was already at level 3 on the special needs register. Neither of these courses of action were implemented. At this stage I started researching alternatives to the school education system as I began to realise that the school system was failing Simon and he was shutting down, and just getting on with being there.

In March 2002, just before Simon's 10th birthday, Channel 4 showed a documentary about different methods of educating children away from school. The daughter of a friend of mine was featured in this programme at the 'Home School' she attended (see Chapter 7) and, as Simon knew her, I allowed him to watch the programme with me.

The next day Simon came to me and said, "Mummy, I don't want to go to school."

My initial response was: "Go to school, I can't cope with this!"

The next day he came to me again and said, "I really don't want to go to school anymore." He had realised from watching the TV programme that he did have a choice. He never went to school again – except to go with me to hand deliver my letter to deregister him from the school.

The previous year I had made contact with the Education Welfare Officer (EWO), who had been very supportive, so I invited him to visit us again. He was very understanding and helpful and he gave me details of a home educator living nearby, who I contacted. This was our first step into the world of Home Education.

Home Education

When I was first considering Home Education, I read that you really need to like your children to be able to spend 24/7 with them. I looked at Simon and thought, "Do I? Can I? I have a stressed, stressy child. Can I live with this 24/7?" However, when he eventually came out of school he was no longer stressed and I loved spending my time with him.

We were at a garden party in the village one afternoon. Simon and I were sitting at a table on our own. Briefly, fleetingly, I thought: "I am sitting all alone," but I soon realised that actually I was with Simon and I was enjoying his company.

My personal experience of education was at a school, in a classroom. But I knew that if I sat Simon at a desk with a piece of paper and a pencil he might as well have been at school – and this would feed into his fear and anxiety. I also knew that if I suggested reading or writing then the shutter would go up and he would refuse to do it, so I didn't force the issue. He would get there in his own time.

"I don't go to school"

In the very beginning, Simon was aware of feeling embarrassed and self-conscious when we went out during the daytime when there were no other children about. He felt that adults were looking at him, judging him, and when we went shopping he was often asked rather flippant questions: *Why are you not at school? Are you playing truant? Are you wagging off school today?*

Simon felt uncomfortable and would say quietly, "I don't go to school."

After a couple of weeks, when Simon was reticent to go out in 'school time', we discussed changing his reply to "I am home educated." This made his response a positive choice rather than defensive negativity.

'I am home educated!'

~ Simon

When Simon used to come home from school, I would ask him what he had done and he would say: "Work, work, work!" in quite a depressed voice. I could see, in my mind, Eeyore, the donkey friend of Winnie the Pooh, and how he would hang his head and look depressed. So, when Simon didn't feel the mental pain or stress he had experienced at school, he did not think he was learning anything. A friend of his asked him what he did for English lessons now he wasn't going to school and his reply was "Nothing." When he repeated this conversation to me, I asked him what language he spoke. We improve our language skills daily through conversation and Simon and I spent a lot of time talking.

Because he didn't feel he was learning anything, as it didn't hurt, I decided to highlight the activities he was doing and their impact on his learning and development. Using a flip chart that I put in his bedroom, I drew a large circle that I sectioned into eight segments. Each segment was labelled according to Gardner's Eight Intelligences: linguistic-verbal, mathematical-logical, visual-spatial, bodily-kinaesthetic, musical, naturalist, interpersonal, and intrapersonal (see chapter 9). Each day we would put something that he had done that day in each segment commensurate with that intelligence. I only needed to do this for a few days before Simon realised that learning didn't need to hurt, and he was able to access his multiple intelligences in many different ways.

Our first contact with the home educating family the EWO had put us in touch with was a visit to their home. The mother and I chatted for a couple of hours while her daughter and Simon played together. We were invited to a group meeting she had organised at Bowood House and Gardens, a beautiful house set in large parklands with a café and extensive children's play area. The following week Simon and I arrived in good time, bought a season ticket and set off to explore and find the others. We had not been there before, so we didn't know our way around. We found the play area, but no one else was there so we returned to the café where we had a drink and some cake. I was nervous and began to feel miserable. I noticed two women with a child of school age, so I approached them and asked if they were part of the group. They were home educators, but not locally; they weren't part of the group I was looking for. I felt like crying. I had taken this massive step to take responsibility for Simon's education and I felt I was failing at the first hurdle. We had come all this way to meet other home educators, but no one was here. Where were they? Eventually we found a couple of local home educating families looking around the house and decided to meet up weekly throughout that summer. Other families joined us and subsequently we were introduced to other groups too. Our adventure had truly begun.

When Simon realised what reading means

By this time, I was running a riding centre that I co-owned and Simon came with me every day. On Saturdays he would help with the other young volunteers, who gave up their weekends to be with the horses and ponies, and during the week I would sometimes let Simon have access to our computer to do whatever he wanted.

One day, as we drove home, I asked Simon what he had learnt that day. His reply was rather a surprise to me. "I've learnt what reading means."

'I've learnt what reading means!'

~ Simon

This sounded rather deep! So I explored his response.

It transpired that he had been playing Pinball on the computer and had discovered the pull-down help menu that explained how to play the game. Suddenly he could see a point to reading, a reason for reading. I explored some more about reading at school and he said that he wasn't interested in the Biff & Chip series of stories at school. In his mind, if that was all reading was about he couldn't see the point, he wasn't interested. Here was the reason for his lack of interest five years earlier: these books had put him off wanting to read. This was a pivotal moment in his learning.

A short while later I discovered a Dorling Kindersley series of interactive books, which are brilliant. They grabbed Simon's attention and we read them together.

The first time I realised he was accessing words easily was during the Harry Potter film 'The Chamber of Secrets' where Harry writes in Tom Riddle's diary. For the first time Simon did not nudge me to read it for him. He was about 12 years old then.

When I told my parents that I was going to home educate Simon their first response was "How can we help?" I was so grateful. Simon had a good relationship with my parents from a very young age and he still called them Nanny and Grampy Ducks. They played an active role and were keen to be involved with Simon's activities.

My mum was a keen kite flyer and at one Home Education meeting she brought along the materials to make simple kites. The whole group joined in and afterwards they enjoyed trying to fly their kites. Simon loved doing crafts with my mum and he learnt wood working and gardening with my father – in fact, this had a long-lasting influence on Simon as he now works as a professional gardener. My father also came over every Thursday to help Simon work through his Electronic Wizard Wonder Boxes: this was a fortnightly correspondence course and Dad learnt about electronics alongside Simon. Dad was also supportive of the Robotics (FLL) team that Simon was an active member of, along with other children from our Home Education group, and he enjoyed going along to competitions to watch them compete.

Sadly, Simon's other grandparents had very little input and from the beginning expressed their disquiet that Simon would only ever end up on the dole! However, about four years later, his grandmother did say that she thought I had done the right thing for Simon.

Since the mid-1980s, my mother's side of the family have been meeting up every August bank holiday for a family gathering, where we play games, share meals and generally catch up from the year before. There are now four generations that meet up. At the first gathering after Simon stopped going to school, several of my aunts and cousins approached me and commented on how different Simon was. Until then, they were not aware he was no longer attending school. This was evidence that I was doing the right thing for him.

Who we met on the way

From that first tentative step into the unknown world of Home Education at Bowood House, we started going regularly to group meetings. The first one was a monthly meeting in Devizes in the scout hall, where we paid a nominal amount to cover the costs. Refreshments were available and some people brought along different activities to share. This is where we made kites with my parents and where we first met Jane and her daughters, Ruby and Ada. (More about them in Chapter 2.)

Jane told us about a group that was about to start in Swindon and about the Yahoo group that was being set up by Shena. We met Shena and her children a short while later at the weekly group meetings in Rodbourne, Swindon. (More about them in Chapter 3.)

We lived on the edge of a very rural village and, even when Simon was at school, he felt somewhat isolated and was reliant on me to take him anywhere. Despite this, we were out and about almost every day doing different things with other families.

At the end of our first summer another family joined us from the same school that Simon had left six months earlier. They lived in the adjacent village to us. This was Heidi and her two boys, Colin and Aidan. (More about them in Chapter 4.)

There were many other families that we met, some regularly, others occasionally, and some that dropped in and out again, but the final family included in this book joined us about 18 months later. This was Mandy and her son, Dan. (More about them in Chapter 5.)

The reason I have chosen to feature these families specifically is because we are still friends now – 17 years later.

Back to Simon's story

These four families all had a positive influence on our time home educating and we met frequently, both at organised events and more casually. The following six years are almost a blur, a whirlwind of activities and events that formed the basis of Simon's life and education, but suffice it to say that we did not stay at home very much. I facilitated his learning and we followed a child-centred autonomous learning process, which literally means that if he showed an interest in something, we pursued it, and if he didn't, we didn't. There is more about what we got up to as a group in Chapter 6.

Significant moments over the next six years

Initially, Simon was too scared to try anything new in case he got it wrong and he insisted that I stayed with him for all activities as he felt so insecure. He was quite introverted and shy, though he felt reasonably comfortable joining in the games with the other children and he was eager to go to the group meetings and events. During school term time it was great for our children to have the ice rink or swimming pool to themselves while the parents chatted in the coffee shop. We would meet every Monday afternoon for swimming and every Wednesday afternoon for ice skating, except when the schools were closed because that was when they were busy. Being home educated gave Simon the freedom to learn at his own speed, in the way he wanted, and to be able to grow and develop emotionally and physically.

Two significant things happened when we were into our third year of home educating. In the May we attended our first Home-Educators Seaside Festival, commonly referred to as HESFES. This was an amazingly magical experience. In excess of 1400 home educating adults and children took over a whole camp site on the Dorset coast. Meeting so many different and diverse people was truly inspirational. Our group from Swindon camped close to each other. Simon went every year thereafter for another six years, either with me or with other members of our Swindon group. He became more confident to be away from me and felt safe with our extended family. He grew very close to the other families included in this book.

Later that same year, Shena and Heidi brought together a group of 11 children to form a team to enter the First Lego League International competition (FLL).

This team brought Simon, James, Colin and Aidan closer together. That first year we were so excited when our team swept through the regional competition; they came fifth in the national competition and qualified to go to the Open European Championship in Eindhoven, where they came 27th out of 52 teams worldwide. Two years later they came third at the national competition, which qualified them to go to the Open Asian Championship in Tokyo. Simon went to Japan with Heidi and her family and was quite happy to go without me. My little lost boy was growing up.

'My little lost boy was growing up.'

~ Susan

Simon's favourite memories were spending time with James and other children, enjoying role playing games in their garden.

After Home Education

As our Home Education journey began drawing to an end, Simon was showing an interest and aptitude in computing and crafts, so we looked through New College's short courses brochure. One of the courses he enrolled in was a textiles evening class, which he loved. They suggested that he could enrol on the A Level Fashion, Design and Textiles course, instead of the GCSE Textiles course, starting in the September of his

16th year, even though at that stage he had no formal qualifications.

We had discussed him attending college full time once he turned sixteen. Other children from our Home Education group were having positive experiences at New College. They appeared to be able to accommodate children who had not come from a school direction. We went along for an interview and he enrolled in the A Level course, as suggested, and he also chose GCSE Photography and an i-media course (a level 1 course in basic computing); the college expected him to do English and maths as well. I suggested that he put a tick against the learning support option. The following year he took a BTech in software development and web design and in his final year he also took a business course.

However, his first day at college was traumatic because all the fear and emotion of school came flooding back. While waiting for the bus, his tummy began to tie into that knot again. His first class was English GCSE, where he was expected to read Shakespeare. When he got home, he was completely stressed out, so I phoned his learning support tutor, Lesley, to say that we had a problem. She immediately took control. "Clearly this is the wrong class for him," she said. The following day she swapped Simon's GCSE Maths and English classes for the Skills for Life classes instead. Suddenly Simon realised he had someone on his side; someone who believed him and was able to take control for him. She was brilliant, so supportive and helped Simon throughout his three years at college.

Dyslexia

In that first year at college Lesley arranged for Simon to be tested for dyslexia and found that he had some dyslexic traits, the worst being his short-term memory. The main consequence of this was that when he looked at the white board, by the time he looked down at his paper he had forgotten what he had seen, hence copying from the board was impossible. Having now been diagnosed with dyslexia he was able to have more classroom assistance and extra time in his exams and also in his driving theory test.

Simon and I did discuss him going on to higher education, university. We agreed that, unless it was a vocational course, it was a burden to start adult life with a massive debt, so he decided he wanted to start working in his own business instead.

After leaving college Simon attended a weekend course on 'Buy to Let', where he took copious notes on his laptop computer and also took a lot of hand-written notes. He was very pleased with himself as this was the first time that he had felt able to take notes without assistance.

Simon Thorley Davies, 27 years old

While Simon was at college he learnt to drive, which ultimately gave him more independence.

During this time my father asked Simon to take on the gardening for him as he was finding it more difficult. Simon had learnt gardening skills from my dad throughout his time being home educated and he continued to care for the garden for Mum after Dad died. Simon also took on the care of his other grandparents' garden and he continued to look after both gardens twice weekly while he set up his own gardening business, GreenFingers, which is now flourishing.

Alongside his own business he shares the care and responsibility of the farm maintenance and animals at our family farm.

His life aim is to generate a passive income by developing his gardening business and building a portfolio of rental and flip properties.

He is passionate about Home Education and he is determined to home educate his own children when the time comes. He also plans to promote Home Education by providing a meeting centre for Home Education groups.

He is a pro-active volunteer and on the steering committee for local charity and community organisations as well as running the Board Gaming Group in the village hall with Aidan.

Simon has useful IT and photography skills and often works on websites and designs leaflets for the volunteer groups as well as his own business.

Working on the farm and doing gardening helps to keep him fit. He is happy and healthy and he can see that he is building the future he wants.

At the start of our Home Education journey I was asked what my aim was for Simon. My reply was that I wanted him to be a happy, well-adjusted, functional adult. This aim could only be fulfilled through time and now Simon is the adult I hoped for.

'It is our choices that show what we truly
are, far more than our abilities.'

~ J.K. Rowling

'The first step toward success is taken
when you refuse to be a captive of the
environment in which you first find yourself.'

~Mark Caine

'You must be the change
that you wish to see in the world.'

~ Gandhi

Chapter 2
Ruby's Story

I took Simon along to our first meeting at Devizes with some trepidation. Who would we meet? What would it be like? Would Simon be able to mix okay?

The meeting was held in a large hall that echoed noisily. The children enjoyed running around, playing in the garden or doing craft activities that had been brought along to share. Simon joined in immediately and clearly was enjoying being with all these children. What a relief.

I first met Jane when she offered to make me a coffee and we then chatted about what had brought each of us to this group. Everyone there was so friendly and I immediately felt welcome and relaxed. Jane told me she ran pottery classes in her home and Simon was welcome to join in. I felt an immediate connection with Jane, and Simon has subsequently developed close friendships with Jane and her two daughters.

Jane's pottery classes were lovely, informal groups, where Jane would demonstrate some techniques and the children would make whatever they wanted. She had a kiln so was able to fire the work to produce finished items.

Jane's story

Jane grew up in the north of England where she attended a Catholic primary school run by very strict nuns who used corporal punishment. Her secondary education was in an all-girls' convent school where she was bored and not inspired by the subjects being taught, except for English. This is probably because Jane is a natural artist and has a flair for all things arts and crafts, which, throughout Jane's adult life, she has developed into a business, producing items she has sold either at craft fairs or, latterly, online. Balancing work and life was challenging and she would often take the children to the markets with her.

Like most of society, Jane believed that school was the right place for children to go to socialise and learn, so she decided to enrol her oldest daughter Ruby in the nearby primary school, where, even though Ruby was already quite advanced in reading and writing, she continued to improve her skills.

'No one can make you feel inferior without your consent.'

~ Eleanor Roosevelt

Ruby's story

Ruby attended school for two years from the age of five, but she was a very shy, introverted child and really did not cope with the noise and being surrounded by people every day, as interactions with most people made her anxious. This anxiety escalated when other children began to bully her and the teachers were irritated because she would get upset easily and was very quiet. Jane realised there was a problem and, though she spoke with the school, nothing changed. Ruby soon became school-phobic – she was scared of everything related to school – so Jane discussed with her the potential options. Then, when Ruby begged Jane to let her stay at home, Jane immediately agreed to let her be home educated. Coming out of school was a monumental relief for Ruby and she now wonders how much her mental health would have suffered if she had stayed in school any longer.

'I feel that I did not fit into the mould that is required to fit into school life.'

~ Ruby

Jane already knew about Home Education, because she had previously lived in a community who had home educated their children. She knew it was legal and had a good idea what she needed to do, though at first she did feel stressed having to deal with outsiders. Like most home educators she learnt the law and was able to quote it when quizzed.

'I had a private education – tailor made.'

~ Ruby

For Ruby, the best thing about being home educated was having freedom. Freedom to follow her own interests and put her time and effort into the things she was truly passionate about. Freedom to be herself, without fear of judgement or being bullied, and was able to choose her own friends, who she could spend one on one time with. This was important for her as an introvert because it was less overwhelming and it enabled her to develop close genuine friendships with the people she felt good connections with. Freedom to sleep or eat as she needed to, which is vital for brain and body development, made the world of difference when it came to concentration and overall wellbeing, and this was incredibly important for Ruby. Freedom to wear clothes that she felt comfortable in, to spend more time outside and have more quality time with her family. This was true freedom.

Ruby found she worked best in the evenings and through the night and so was able to get up late in the mornings feeling refreshed. She was able to follow her own body clock.

Ruby attended many Home Education meet ups where we often did activities together – arts and crafts were her favourite and she often joined in with things like tie dyeing, drawing and painting, model building, pottery, making collages, weaving, sewing, candle making and so on.

She also enjoyed the music group (especially playing guitar and drums), swimming, skating, visiting places like museums and animal sanctuaries, history events, festivals, nature reserves, and general social meet ups. Learning was very organic, through everyday life, where everything and everywhere was presented as a learning opportunity, 24/7. Nothing was categorised into specific subjects and Ruby enjoyed the freedom to follow her own interests and to learn spontaneously. Nothing was classed as work.

The term 'unschooling' would most accurately describe her experience, where she was in control of her own education and chose what she wanted to learn.

She enjoyed learning life skills. She helped look after the home and became proficient at cooking, sewing and using appliances. She was encouraged to manage her own money and became more independent indoors and outdoors, doing basic DIY and animal and child care.

She enjoyed learning how to learn: how to think for herself and seek out information she was genuinely interested in. Many topics were covered this way and she developed a well-rounded understanding of most subjects, her favourites being English and art. Ruby felt that all her needs were met and interests facilitated by being home educated.

The one thing Ruby felt uncomfortable about was when adults would quiz her – usually with maths questions. Being put on the spot would make most children feel vulnerable.

When Ruby reached the age of about fifteen or sixteen, she was becoming an independent person, able to choose her own path in life. She chose not to go to college and instead found work babysitting, drawing tattoo designs and working in a local clothes shop.

'I enjoyed learning how to learn.'

~ Ruby

Ada is Jane's youngest child and by the time she was of school age she was happy to be home educated alongside Ruby and chose not to go to school.

Jane found that Ada's ability to learn was very different to Ruby, as she struggled with reading and writing, so Jane went on a course about dyslexia and realised that Ada was dyslexic and also that she was a kinaesthetic learner, which means she learns best through feel rather than listening or seeing (more about this in Chapter 9). Through the different activities and techniques that Jane learnt on this course she was able to help and guide Ada to learn in different ways and to access words more easily.

Life was busy and sometimes difficult, but Jane knew she had ultimately made the right decisions for her children.

Ruby May Patricia Craven, 29 years old

Ruby met Marly and developed a stable relationship with him, and when their family came along she knew she would follow a similar Home Education path with their children. Her children are now six and eight and are enjoying the same freedom that their mother clearly thrived on. She has a wonderful supportive partner and family and friends from all walks of life and surrounds the family with a lovely community of other home educators.

Ruby feels she is lucky to be supported emotionally and financially by her partner. She worked before she had her children and is now planning to fulfil her lifetime ambition to be self-employed, starting her own business making and selling handmade items.

Her family are all in good health and they follow a vegan diet because this is the best way to control their son's allergies.

Ruby still enjoys learning new things while continuing to pursue her interests of walking, being in and studying nature, reading, music, cooking, art, crafts, history, and yoga – but most importantly, she is happy and always trying to better herself. She prides herself on being compassionate and kind, honest and open-minded. She now considers being home educated a gift, as it made her who she is today in the best way possible. She is her own person, a functioning member of society, with essential life skills and the ability to cope in many different situations. She learns new things of her own accord and can think for herself, and she and Marly are raising their children in a loving and respectful way, so they are also kind, compassionate and happy people.

'Doing what you like is freedom.
Liking what you do is happiness.'

~ Frank Tyger

'Through my education, I didn't just
develop skills, I didn't just develop the
ability to learn, but I developed confidence.'

~ Michelle Obama

'If you have the courage to begin,
you have the courage to succeed.'

~ David Viscott

Chapter 3
James's Story

By the time we went along to the weekly Rodbourne meetings, organised by Shena, I was more confident and by now knew a few more families. In the same way as other group meetings, we paid a nominal amount to cover costs for the hall and refreshments. This is where Simon first met James and his older sibling, who is the same age as Simon.

Shena was immediately friendly and supportive, understanding the issues that had caused Simon so much anxiety. She invited Simon to join James at the church youth club that she ran weekly in the same hall. Simon enjoyed going to this group, though he insisted that I stayed there with him, so I sat in the corner and he wouldn't even let me go across the road to the shop. It took a few more months for Simon to feel confident enough for me to leave him for a short time.

Shena's Home education group grew quite quickly, with many families from in and around Swindon meeting regularly.

Shena's story

Shena had decided to embrace Home Education when she left secondary school. Though she'd had a reasonable school experience herself, she could see the short fall of the education system.

She had read an article about Home Education at Lower Shaw Farm in Swindon and the origin of Education Otherwise, which is now a national organisation for home educators. Shena joined Education Otherwise shortly after her first child was born and subsequently became the local representative. She joined email lists and actively went looking for home educators in Swindon, where she and her family lived.

Shena's decision to home educate was based on her own philosophical reasons and, as this was a life choice, Shena commenced her child-centred autonomous learning from the beginning.

Her eldest child did attend school for one term, at the age of eight, just to experience it, but after one term decided not to go anymore. Otherwise neither of Shena's children attended school. Her youngest child, James, was happy being home educated and was not interested in experiencing school.

Shena was an Open University tutor, worked part time in IT and also did freelance work from home and she would get up really early to do her work before the children woke. This enabled her to have free time with her children as required. She found that being in education helped her to facilitate the family life balance.

Shena knew the law and was our 'go to' person when we needed advice on how to deal with the authorities.

Why can't we just go with what people have a feel for?'

~ Shena

James's story

James never felt the urge to go to school. He was quite happy being educated at home and he enjoyed joining in with the groups and meeting different people and, in fact, from a very early age he happily associated with the adults and other children he met at the church the family attended regularly.

As Shena followed a totally child-led philosophy, both children were able to follow their own interests. Her oldest child was de-coding letters at a very early age, while James could spell at about three years old, though his reading skills came later.

Shena soon realised that both her children were beyond Key Stage 1 level before they were of school age, which reinforced her belief in her methods of education.

At a young age, James didn't like being left on his own with strangers away from Shena but was happy to be part of the Home Education group, as he liked the people he met there and enjoyed their company. He also enjoyed a diverse range of activities alongside all the Home Education meetings he attended.

He got frustrated when adults would ask him what year he was in, as this question has no point of reference to a home educated child. He would answer with his age and later on was able to add the school year he thought it related to.

James is an accomplished musician in recorder, guitar and saxophone, which he learnt by attending the Swindon Young Musicians (SYM) that ran classes on Saturday mornings. Simon also went along for a short while, to learn guitar.

Having free access to the internet, James was able to satisfy his curiosity by researching his interests. He enjoyed YouTube videos and learnt problem solving through a video series on games design. He learnt a lot from the internet and reading books. These skills helped him when the FLL team was set up by Shena when she bought James a Lego Mindstorm kit. In the team each child gravitated to their interests; where Simon enjoyed the robot design and performance, James preferred the programming and computer work involved with it and enjoyed doing the research work for the group project.

James had an interest in Pokémon and, when Dan joined the group, they became close friends through this mutual hobby. The Pokémon games taught them life lessons and attitudes about compassion and caring that they enjoyed sharing with friends.

James felt a bit torn when his parents separated, He chose to spend his time equally with them and was able to continue joining in all his activities. James went swimming, ice skating and rock climbing. He also went to pottery classes with Jane and, of course, his family went to HESFES. His outdoor activities included visiting Lower Shaw Farm, attending Forest School, a one-day workshop at the Braeside Centre in Devizes, which provides tailor-made learning events, and our group meetings throughout the summer at Lydiard Park.

Shena and her children had Russian lessons from a tutor because, for a number of years, Shena's family hosted some visiting children from Belarus, who came over, through a charity, for holidays and to access cleaner air and good food. We also hosted two boys one summer.

James realised he is a goal-orientated learner and, at 14, he started several Open University (OU) courses and ultimately attained 210 points towards his entrance to university.

When his older sibling went to university and then Dan and Simon went to New College, James felt their loss, even though he was still attending Home Education groups and continuing with the FLL competition, where new members had joined the team.

The one thing James, Simon, Colin and Aidan all agree they missed out on through being home educated was the timetabled structure of formal institutions and the lack of repetitive practice that they needed to be able to do once they went into structured learning. James felt that, as Home Education was mostly self-motivating, he may have been able to use his time better, although he was proactive within the groups.

After Home Education

Though James had attained enough points for university entrance through OU courses, Bristol University required him to do A Level Maths for the engineering course he wanted to do. He attended New College to get this qualification, which enabled him to enrol for his degree course.

James found digs in Bristol and enjoyed a good student life. He joined the Christian Union and attended church regularly, where he was confirmed. Through the Christian Union he joined others who went out at night to give water and help to people coming out of the pubs and clubs. This is called Club Loving. James would also talk with homeless people on the streets and realised that there is a lot we can learn from them. He has found that he likes to help other people.

James did have some struggles with his course work at university but has now completed a Bachelor's degree in engineering.

James La Fleur, 24 years old

Shortly after finishing university, James started a job he enjoys as a remote IT support for BUPA Dental Care. This gives him financial independence and with his mother's help he is now buying his own home in Bristol, as he has decided that the rent that he has been paying out can go toward a mortgage.

James has made some significant lifestyle choices through his time at university and more so now that he is in full time work. He started looking into himself and realised that he had been too self-absorbed. He is now able to recognise when he feels angry or emotional and potentially why, which enables him to deal with his feelings rather than bottling them.

With this ability to recognise emotions within himself, he has become more aware of how to behave in company and has more clarity of communication by listening and being interruptible. He is aware that the people we are close to accept us for who we are and accept when we are maybe less polite.

Like most students he has smoked and drank occasionally, but now he is considering embracing being a vegetarian as he enjoys cooking and is conscious of wanting to improve his health. He regularly attends a gym and finds stimulation from the focus and engagement of doing the exercises. This helps him with his physical and emotional well-being.

Shena's family used bicycles frequently and James still uses his bike today as a means of transport, which helps to keep him in general good health and fitness.

More recently he has started to recognise potential autistic tendencies in himself. However, he does not want to define himself as such, as over classifying oneself is not appropriate or really helpful. He feels that his association with the people he met through university, his church and especially Home Education and his experiences with them have helped him to be who he is today. He feels close to all his family members. Simon is his longest standing friend, and he has had continuous friendships with Dan, Colin and Aidan. As a result of being home educated together, they are all still close friends today. James is happy in mixed company and also likes to be on his own, as he enjoys his own space.

'Excellence is the enemy of the good.'

~ James

'Proactivity is better even if it doesn't always go the way you want.'

~ James

'It is paradoxical that many educators and parents still differentiate between a time for learning and a time for play without seeing the vital connection between them.'

~ Leo Buscaglia

'Life itself is your teacher, and you are in a
state of constant learning.'

~ Bruce Lee

'Just keep taking chances
and having fun.'

~ Garth Brooks

Chapter 4
Colin and Aidan's Stories

Heidi and her two boys, Colin and Aidan, turned up at the Rodbourne group meeting in September of the same year that Simon started being home educated. We soon realised we lived in adjacent villages and that the boys had all attended the same school but in different years, though we had never met until then.

My first memory of Colin and Aidan is them sitting across from each other playing a board game. They were quite quiet and didn't mingle well at that stage, but they soon came out of themselves and joined in with playing with the other children.

Heidi immediately became an active member of our Home Education group and was well liked by everyone. She often took Simon with them to the robotics (FLL) group and took care of him when the team went to Japan; he would also go with her family to HESFES.

Heidi & Tony's story

Heidi and her husband Tony grew up in South Africa and

I enjoyed chatting with her about the differences and similarities in our lives during the 1970s.

Heidi and Tony had decided to move to Britain because they thought it was a better place to bring up a family.

When Colin was very young they recognised that he was very bright so they looked for an appropriate school that would nurture his intelligence and accelerate him through the curriculum, commensurate to his ability. This brought them to settle in the village close to Swindon.

Heidi had been interested in Home Education and the year before they embarked on it, she and Tony had visited Shena to find out more. Heidi did a lot of research, read books and learnt more about Education Otherwise. She was keen to be more involved with her children's education.

By the time Colin was seven he had already joined the year above his age group, but the new headmistress wanted him to rejoin his own age group and did not want to keep him with his educational peers. This would mean he would be repeating Year 3. At this point Heidi and Tony agreed to spend the summer holidays experimenting with Home Education and to decide at the end of the summer whether or not the boys would go back to school.

Both Heidi and Tony had well paid jobs, but Heidi's contract was coming to an end, so she decided to stop working to spend her time with the children. They started with some lessons using educational computer programmes and the children chose what they wanted to do. This continued for about a year as the lessons slowly, naturally phased out. There was never a rigid structure and they didn't feel they needed to replicate school as they trusted the Home Education process. They allowed their children supervised exposure to the internet, which they felt was better than restricted protection. They were never afraid of Home Education but embraced it to the full and they both felt supported by the other members of our Home Education community.

'We all live with the objective of being happy; our lives are all different and yet the same.'

~ Anne Frank

Colin's story

Colin was deciphering written words before he was two years old and demonstrated his ability to see patterns easily. He was a logical thinker from a very young age. I remember having quite a deep conversation with him about evolution versus creationism when he was about eight.

Colin remembers that he experienced some bullying in his first two years at school; however, he mostly had a good school experience, especially when he was accelerated to Year 3, as he was the class teacher's favourite, but he has no regrets about leaving school to be home educated. While at school Colin did not feel educationally challenged and he now realises that he was also not very socially aware and was easily manipulated during this time.

Being home educated presented many more opportunities to pursue his interests and learn in unconventional ways. He was free to do what he wanted – and he was still learning. Learning was happening and he was having fun. He had the ability to choose who he interacted with and was able to find people to share activities with. He felt that, though there may have been some things he missed out on by not going to school, it was completely outweighed by what he did do.

'Learning happens when having fun.'

~ Colin

Heidi shared mentoring the FLL team with Shena, and Colin became an active member of the team when he was ten. He enjoyed the computer programming for the robot performance on the challenge mat.

At home he had free access to a computer and enjoyed playing games. Through RuneScape he learnt a lot about real life and he had a rich social interaction through the games. Colin feels that his online interaction is as valuable as his offline interaction and he continues to interact online today, often with Simon, Aidan and other members of our Home Education group. Colin even met up with one of his online friends when they were at HESFES at the same time.

Colin became an accomplished pianist and he enjoyed drama classes, where he attained a Lamda Gold Medal in public speaking. He enjoyed the collaborative experience of role-playing games with his family and friends. This involved planning and developing the storyline, including the individual characters for each participant. He now considers this form of interaction the best social activity he is involved in. Colin drew comic characters and stories in great detail. One day he would like to be a games designer.

His family joined in with the regular Home Education activities, including swimming, ice skating, rock climbing and group meetings. He enjoyed a weaving workshop and Horse Ownership course.

Colin started doing Open University courses at 14 as an alternative to GCSEs and A Levels. Even though the courses had deadlines, he enjoyed the freedom to work on each assignment to his own time scale. He completed a first class honours degree by the time he was 18. As he completed the degree at home through the Open University, he realised he had missed out on the university experience, which is why he decided to attend Holloway University in London to do a master's degree. When he started attending university he found it challenging to be in a structured system with deadlines, even though he had worked to deadlines with the Open University.

Colin Putman, 24 years old

Colin is enjoying the experience of student life and is continuing his education by doing a PhD in Information Security at the same university.

Since going to university, Colin has become more self-reliant; he now feels he has more self-awareness and describes himself as openly gender fluid. He is happy with his wide circle of friends from the Home Education group, university and other communities that he mixes with and though he feels he lacks fitness, he does enjoy walking.

Aidan's story

Aidan is Colin's younger brother and he has very little memory of the year he spent at school; his memories are neither good nor bad: he thinks it was an okay experience. He remembers being asked by his parents if he would like to be home educated while they were trialling it with Colin over the summer holidays and he was quite happy to continue once the new school year began.

At home, Aidan was able to concentrate on things he enjoyed and avoid things he was not interested in. He absorbed knowledge everywhere and learned a lot; sometimes it was conscious learning and other times it just happened. He had the ability to pursue his interests and learn in unconventional ways. He had the freedom to do what he wanted and was still learning in the process.

As a young child Aidan was easily provoked and sometimes showed his anger as he struggled with needing to control the games and activities with the other children, which they wouldn't always allow. Heidi was very even-tempered and would take Aidan to one side and quietly talk with him about his behaviour. Otherwise Aidan generally joined in and mixed with the other children at the group meetings. Heidi would join him and Colin in the swimming pool and on the ice rink because they were too young at the beginning and needed supervision.

He and his brother joined in with all the activities and they enjoyed dabbling in lots of things, including badminton, rock climbing, pottery, drama and trainee horse whispering.

Aidan joined in with the frequent robotics sessions leading toward the FLL competitions even though he was initially too young to compete with the other members of the team. He enjoyed being involved with the programming and the research projects. This held him in good stead when he was old enough to be part of the team and he was the lead programmer when they went to Japan to compete in the Open Asian Championship. Being part of this team gave him a strong grounding in team work.

Aidan actively enjoyed playing all sorts of games, role-playing and reading. He is now very good at being the 'games master' in games like Dungeons and Dragons, where he is in charge of guiding, controlling and teaching the game to other participants. The family frequently enjoyed playing board games and built up a big library of interesting games. Aidan learnt the games organically through being exposed to them from a young age and actively participating.

I remember the first time I played 'Go' with his family at a 'Go' meeting in a pub nearby. It is a game for two people, and I was playing with Aidan. As I took my turn, he would tell me about the game and the best moves or the implication of each move. I really felt that I was barely holding my own against him, so, when I made a move that I thought was okay, but actually proved to be very good and basically beat his game, he was really upset, and I felt awful. This was not the only time I played 'Go' with Aidan and I did not have such a resounding victory again.

Aidan has been studying with the Open University since his early teens. He has taken a wide range of courses commensurate with his interests, so his first degree is taking a little longer to complete. He enjoyed being alone and self-regulated in his learning as, though it was a solitary process, he was proactive and motivated to study the courses he had chosen.

In retrospect, Aidan believes the school practice of repetitive work and copious writing might have improved his speed when taking written exams. He found he was not as quick as he needed to be when given a time constraint to complete a piece of work.

Aidan Putman, 22 years old

Aidan has almost completed his first degree, through the Open University, and he plans to go on to university to study maths and physics, as he enjoys the logic of mathematics.

'Play is the highest form of research.'

~ Albert Einstein

He still reads for entertainment and continues to enjoy board games. He is a keen games player and he can easily learn the rules and explain them well to new players. This is a useful skill, as both Aidan and Simon are organisers and members of a local board gaming group. Aidan is also a member of the local "Go" group with his brother, Colin and father, Tony. He is often the 'games master' for the Dungeons and Dragons tournaments they play online every Sunday afternoon in a group including Simon, Colin and two other people who were part of their Home Education group.

Aidan is much more aware of himself now and he does not allow his emotions to control him; he is more mature and has more self-discipline.

So, from that young boy who became frustrated when he wanted to control the other children, he has been able to channel his skills into being a very effective games master.

He says he doesn't do enough exercise and could be a bit fitter. Otherwise he is a healthy, well-rounded person with a fun sense of humour.

'Your time is limited, so don't waste it living someone else's life.'

~ Steve Jobs

Chapter 5
Dan's Story

Mandy and Dan

About a year after Heidi and her boys started home educating, Mandy and her son, Dan, joined us at the Rodbourne group meetings and became regular members of our Home Education group. For the last two years Mandy had been concerned that Dan's easy going, kind and protective nature was being taken advantage of at school. He was becoming aggressive and defensive and he was often angry when he came home.

Things would settle down during the holidays, but the anger and aggression re-emerged when he returned to school again.

During those two years Mandy researched the law thoroughly, but she put off removing him from school because her main concern was finding other families who were also home educating. Dan was very sociable and enjoyed mixing with other people, so she needed to find out if and where there were groups that Dan could join.

Through her research online and on the advice of a friend she discovered Education Otherwise. She was delighted to discover that she and Dan literally walked passed the home of the local representative, Shena, on their way to school and even more delighted to find out there was a weekly Home Education meeting across the road from the school. Unknowingly, she had been walking past us for two years!

Mandy's story

Mandy is the oldest child of a large family and, growing up, she felt responsible for her younger siblings and would help look after them. She is very much a people person and loves helping others, sometimes to her own detriment.

When Mandy first wanted to embrace Home Education, Dan's father, Pete, was uncertain and concerned that Dan would not get what he needed if he didn't attend school. Pete's father, Dan's grandfather, lived nearby and his belief was that Dan needed to go to school to learn how to deal with bullies.

Once Mandy had decided to take Dan out of school, she gave up work and other activities, except for her regular choir meetings, so she could devote her time to Dan's education.

It wasn't long before Pete could see how Home Education was benefitting Dan and he became more supportive, emotionally as well as financially. They especially enjoyed being able to spend more time together as a family.

*'Home Education is
un-incarcerated education.'*

~ Mandy

Dan's story

Dan went to school until he was ten and for the most part he was quite tense, especially in the last two years. He was always on edge, waiting to see what would happen next. He found the teachers were unfair, especially when he was being bullied by other children – one child in particular – and if he retaliated, he would get into trouble. Mostly he would find himself intercepting conflicts between other children; he was the champion of the weaker children who were being picked on and this meant that he was always on the alert. As time went on Mandy became the brunt of his vexation; he was generally quiet and well behaved while at school, but he would shout at her when he came home. Mandy noticed, with sadness, that Dan's natural curiosity and joyful nature had quietened and all but disappeared. Dan had built an emotional wall and learnt to shield himself from the stress of the other children and their interactions. He described being at school as 'surviving' and said being at home was 'living'.

*'School was about surviving whereas home
was about living.'*

~ Dan

Throughout Dan's first day of being home educated he kept asking Mandy, in wonderment, if he really didn't have to go to school anymore.

When Dan first left school he only wanted to mix with children of the same age as himself and he did miss the company of two children in particular. (Even though they lived nearby he only reconnected with them when he was older and attending New College.) Within the Home Education group, he soon linked up with James, as he lived close by and they had common interests, especially Pokémon. My son Simon and Dan didn't like each other at first, because they reflected each other's issues from school. However, as they both grew more confident through Home Education, they became more tolerant of each other and are now best friends along with James.

Dan had a fear of being misunderstood so he actively learnt how to interpret people and understand them. He felt drawn to helping people to explore their emotions, as he was doing himself. Through Home Education he was able to have the emotional and physical space that he needed to find himself.

Mandy used Dan's interests to engage him in learning. She used his Yu-Gi-Oh! trading cards to represent different grammatical meanings, amongst other things. Dan joined in with the weekly group meetings and activities alongside the other families, including swimming, trampolining and camping at HESFES. He was able to follow his interests of astrology, archery, manga drawing and the African drumming that his parents brought along to the Home Education group.

'The universe is full of magical things, patiently waiting for our wits to grow sharper.'

~ Eden Phillpotts

As he was a kinaesthetic learner, being home educated enabled Dan to explore a pleasing lifestyle balance of home, friends and learning. He felt free, safe and happy as he was able to be himself and do what he wanted. He learnt social patience and he found himself without fear or worry of being judged. He no longer felt the claustrophobia that had denied him his emotional space, and his learning was happening naturally through living, interacting and conversing.

When Dan was 14, my son Simon started at New College and James was busy taking Open University courses. Dan missed the regular interactions, so he decided to go to New College to meet more people. As he was under 16, his parents were required to fund his courses. He returned to college after he turned 16 and again when he was 18, and took some GCSE qualifications.

Dan Parsons, 25 years old

Since leaving college, Dan has had several jobs in retail and he has also earnt some money by streaming games online. He was beginning to pick up quite a good following but as he worked mostly in the late evening and into the night he had to stop as he was disturbing the rest of the household.

During these years of work and seeking employment Dan has been able to grow into himself and mature. He has a keen insight into life and himself and has evolved into a more understanding, respectful and sympathetic adult. He is planning to take a new approach to his work life balance, as he wants to be more self-reliant, and he plans to move somewhere where he can achieve this aim.

Dan works continually to improve his emotional, mental, physical and spiritual health. Living with Mandy has given him a very clear understanding of nutrition as Mandy has evolved her vegetarianism and become an expert in raw foods and vegan diet. Dan now follows a vegan regime with his parents, both for health reasons and to address his food intolerances.

'All the wonders you seek are within yourself.'

~ Thomas Browne

Dan is aware of his own intelligence and feels that associating with a "world of dummies", as he puts it, is pointless, so he is drawn to helping people to help themselves and chooses who he socialises with. He is discerning about who his friends are, and Simon and James are the strongest and most reinforced friendships he has. Dan describes all his relationships as having 'string' or 'chain' links: some are stronger than others, and some are unbreakable links. He regularly joins Simon and Aidan for board gaming evenings, and he has a weekly three-way online chat with James and Simon, which reinforces their friendships. He is also considering becoming a lodger in James' house in Bristol.

Dan recognises that it is better to have money working for him rather than him working for money and he is striving to achieve this by becoming his own boss. Dan's end game is to settle down and continue to have fun and be flexible.

Section 2

Insight into Home Education

'Only put off to tomorrow what you are
willing to die having left undone.'

~ Pablo Picasso

'The greatest discovery of all time is that
a person can change his future by merely
changing his attitude.'

~ Oprah Winfrey

Chapter 6
What Happened and Where

Once Simon was no longer attending school and we launched into Home Education it soon became clear that learning and learning opportunities were already available in our lives. There was no differentiation between the activity of Home Education and the day to day living of our active life. Today this is referred to as 'radical unschooling'; however, I prefer to think of it as a Radical Lifestyle, where we are able to follow our own path. In this chapter I take you through the elements of our Radical Home Education, or radical lifestyle, by describing the different places our life took us and what we did when we got there.

When I first decided to home educate Simon, I had no idea where to begin. Where would we start out on our learning discovery? Where could we go to find other families who were following the same path? I think this is the biggest fear of parents embarking on this diverse route of education: that little voice that questions your decision, your ability and tells you that you might get it wrong.

If you're considering home educating, you may be asking yourself: "Do we need a classroom at home?"

The answer is no. A dedicated space for the child to have their computer, develop their interests, and spread out their projects is useful, but the kitchen or dining room table is just as suitable.

Simon had enough room in his bedroom for his own computer and a table where he was able to leave his Electronic Wizard boxes and contents laid out from one session to the next.

Shena and Heidi, who had brought together the FLL team of 11 keen children, held most of the robotics meetings in Shena's rather large kitchen and sometimes they met at Heidi's home. Following one session Simon was so fired up by the design of the robot that he sat at our dining table, way past midnight that same evening, working on an attachment for one of the tasks.

Other members of our home educating group also used their homes for home educating activities. Jane ran pottery classes in her living room, where she provided the clay and gave instruction. She also had the facility for firing the items, which were then glazed by the children at later meetings. Another family hosted a music club at their home, where there was a set of drums and various instruments to enable the children to play as a band or group.

*'Life is what happens
when you're busy making other plans.'*

~ John Lennon

Some of our group meetings were held in church or local community halls, which would attract a nominal charge to cover the costs. At these meetings we did whatever activities were brought along by each family. Some families also met at a local farm, Lower Shaw Farm, which was open to the public. They also sometimes ran workshops there, in circus tricks or basket weaving.

During the summer months we would arrange a variety of outdoor meetings. A few times we spent the day walking up to one of the chalk white horses on the Wiltshire Downs; we would take a picnic and have a group lunch on the hill. It felt like we were on top of the world. I love the rolling downs of Wiltshire.

We met at Lydiard Park, which is a beautiful parkland on the edge of Swindon. I have fond memories of it from when I was a child and it was where my parents would take Simon when he was very young to feed the ducks.

In the centre of Swindon is a formal garden called Queen's Park where we met occasionally and we also went to Bowood House, which had a wonderful climbing structure that was well liked by the children. We were lucky to have quite a few local places where we could meet and the children could run around and play together.

I also organised some visits to my field where the families could meet my horses and ponies, explore the bluebell woodland adjacent to my land and discover wildlife in the pond.

I have wonderful memories of the days when I had up to 17 people, a mixture of children and adults, all playing and interacting with my horses. Each session I would split them into groups of three and allocate one of the horses or ponies to each group. The groups would include someone more experienced with my horses to help the 'newbies'. I would show them how to interact with their horse and get the horse to follow and stop with the handler. I called this "The Trainee Horse Whispering" class.

Another fun visit to my field was when we had an artist come to teach us how to do charcoal drawings of moving animals. My horses and ponies were very obliging, and it was so funny when Rhidian, my black cob, stood directly in front of Jane. He was almost saying "Draw me!"

Simon had been given an old car that we kept at the field and, being careful of the horses, he practised driving around the land to get the feel of a car. Later he learnt how to tow and reverse a trailer around the farm using my Land Rover. I gave him every opportunity to practise this skill before he eventually took to the road when he was 17.

As well as the group-organised activities, we also arranged visits to many places of interest. We had a private showing of the Wroughton Aircraft Museum where we heard about the first airplane designs, saw the first commercial planes ever used, and learned about the Irish linen that was used to cover the wings to make them lighter. We were also taught how to make paper darts and we had a competition to see whose would go the furthest.

When Swindon was developing to the north, the builders came across an old Roman site, which they opened up for school groups to explore. We were able to access a day workshop, where they told us what they had found there, gave the children an experience of excavating a mock site and enabled them to do a rubbing using a piece of paper and a wax crayon.

The University of Bath in Swindon ran a series of lectures, aimed at school children, that Shena was able to get us access to. Our group filled the first two rows and the children showed a lot of interest in the topics being presented.

Wherever you live, there will be farms, museums, parkland and other sites suitable for group meetings and activities, and lots of places that you can visit. Today the internet is a great source of inspiration.

'Education, therefore, is a process of living and not a preparation for future living.'

~ John Dewey

At HESFES

The first HESFES (Home Educators Seaside Festival)

that we went to was absolutely magical. This is where about 1400 home educators and their families took over a whole camp site in Charmouth, Dorset. A group of us camped close to each other and we sometimes shared meals and activities. Simon joined up with two other children and they rode their bikes around the camp site, happily doing their own thing. Each morning some of us would meet at the Purple People Eater café for a fun breakfast where we were led in discussion about all sorts of controversial ideas and concepts.

Each day there were different activities going on in the main marquee, from music to science, and various conferences on different educational concepts. My one memory of a science talk was a young lad, about seven years old, clearly deaf, who was sitting on the edge of the low stage, discussing the theory of quantum mechanics with the person on the stage. This is the beauty of Home Education.

Other activities that were organised throughout the week included archery, leatherwork, felting, willow weaving and many more that I have now forgotten.

Late one evening, when Simon had not returned to the caravan, I went to look for him. One family of our group was parked over the other side of the camp site and Simon was over there with them. We proceeded to stay there, around their camp fire, until about 1am in the morning. As we walked back across the site to our caravan there were huddles of teenagers and if this had been Swindon high street or the middle of any town or city, I would have felt very intimidated by them. Here, in the middle of HESFES, full of home educated children, there was no feeling of fear or intimidation because it wasn't 'us and them', we were one big family.

At the end of the week there was a fancy dress parade and a concert by anyone who wanted to be included. One young lad took a tin can on the stage and stood on it balanced on one leg. There were many inventive entries.

This was an annual event that was held at different sites. I went with Simon for the first three years and after that he went with either Mandy and her family or Heidi and her family. They would all camp near each other and have a communal tent.

~~~

When I started listing all the activities we did and the diversity of them I was amazed. I want to share with you what we did, where and how, but I don't want to just give you a list, so here I will describe the activities under different headings: physical activities, creativity, academic pursuits and social awareness. I've also included a section on the robotics team (FLL) that became such a huge part of some of our children's lives.

Some of the activities were regular and others were one-off events, but you can see that we always had something to do and we were always busy. Learning was mostly an incidental by-product: it just happened.

Physical Activities

Luckily for us Swindon had a good swimming pool – The Oasis – and an ice rink – The Link, where there was also a climbing wall facility. Our group would access both these facilities weekly. Monday afternoon was swimming and Wednesday afternoon was ice skating. Both sports centres had good cafés for the after-activity chats and for those of us who did not join in. At that time Swindon Council produced annual membership cards that offered a discount for the centres. This enabled the children to access these facilities at a reduced cost. The climbing wall was also accessed for a daily short course over one week, which Simon, Colin and Aidan returned to on other occasions. Rock climbing encourages teamwork and trust.

We all enjoyed playing badminton at another sports hall in Swindon, where we had the hall and courts to ourselves. We were able to help the children learn a new skill and have fun playing with each other, individually or in pairs.

The one-off events were attended by most of the children. One of our favourite events was a tailor-made day at the Braeside Education and Conference Centre near Devizes. Both adults and children participated, and we were put into teams that started at a different challenge. The challenges required physical activity and problem-solving skills that encouraged teamwork and an element of competition.

Riding a bicycle is a useful skill and some of the children successfully participated in a course to attain their Cycling Proficiency certificates.

Trampolining was a popular pastime and some of the children went to classes at the local sports centres and subsequently had their own trampolines.

The owners at Lower Shaw Farm organised circus tricks workshops, which were run weekly. Simon enjoyed learning to use the diablo, devil sticks and poi. My mother enjoyed joining us with her poi.

Creativity

This heading covers a very wide and diverse range of interests and skills, from music to yarn crafts, pottery to drawing and many more in between.

Music and drama

Our group brought a lot of music and instruments to our gatherings. Besides learning different instruments at Swindon Young Musicians, we also learnt to play the Djembe in drumming classes run by Mandy and Pete; both Simon and Dan enjoyed this immensely.

At HESFES, Jane and Heidi often instigated a singsong around the camp fire. They played their guitars and we joined in singing late into the evening.

Simon enjoyed attending Stagecoach Performing Arts, where he pursued dance, singing and acting. He was also a member of their agency and was sent for some auditions.

One Christmas, Simon and a few of the others joined in the 'Christmas on Ice' show that was an annual event at the Link Centre ice rink.

Arts and crafts

Jane is a natural, skilled artist and as well as her pottery classes, she also encouraged model making at our hall groups. She would bring along different materials and ideas for each session.

Colin was very skilled in drawing intricate comic stories, Dan loved doing Manga drawings and we all enjoyed drawing charcoal pictures of my horses.

We were able to access some art projects, funded through Wiltshire County Council, that we arranged especially for our Home Education group. The first project was over two days near Marlborough, where the children made plasticine models, discussed a story line using these models and then got the plasticine models to 'act out' the story while each frame was photographed to make a 3D stop motion animation video. It was fun to see the story develop and watch the finished film. It gave us a greater appreciation of the Wallace and Gromit films.

The second project was also over two days, in my local village hall. This was with a weaving tutor, who supplied us with materials and different types of looms. Each morning she would discuss and demonstrate the different weaving techniques. The group used peg looms, rake looms, frames made from twigs or straws and different fabrics and yarns. She was impressed with the way the home educated children were so proactive and imaginative in comparison to other school groups she had been involved with.

Simon, my mum and I joined some spinning, weaving and dying guilds, where we learnt how to spin and process our own alpaca fleeces. These yarn crafts sparked Simon's interest and he went on a textiles evening class at New College, which then enabled him to take an A Level in Fashion Design and Textiles. At Lower Shaw Farm we attended a basket weaving day course where we learnt basic willow weaving and made some sculptures for the plants in the garden.

Academic Pursuits

Each family had a different approach to academic learning depending on the individual child.

Language is very important and even when Simon was a baby I always spoke to him using my normal language, not simplified baby talk. I would also use an adjective in front of the noun. For example, I would say the colour of his clothes as well as the name of the item, or ask for his left or right foot for his brown shoe or blue sock. Another time, when he was about three years old, I encouraged a basic mathematical process by asking him to feed the guinea pigs by giving them one scoop of feed for each guinea pig in the cages. This is a simple task in correlation.

When I first started home educating Simon I proactively sought different ways to access words and reading. I wanted to make it fun and interesting, so I found various games that were based on words. I think our favourite one was called Cats, Dogs and Hogs. I would allow Simon to use the dictionary to access his words.

Another of our fun activities was listing the different words that describe roads as we drove along – road, street, avenue, lane, to name but a few. There are surprisingly many options, even more so in different areas of the country. Simon would do a tally of how many he saw of each one and add any new ones to the list. My plan was to expand on this activity into making graphs or charts of the data, though this didn't actually happen.

I allowed Simon free access to his computer and showed him a very useful button called Spell Check. Simon is quite fastidious and getting the spelling correct was and still is very important to him.

I would always describe things like cutting the toast in half or quarters; cutting a pizza into eight pieces, and so on. Simon understood this at a basic level. However, one day, when we were discussing his party and how many pizzas we needed to feed everyone, he suddenly had a realisation about fractions, that the number at the bottom indicated the number of pieces the whole was divided into. Learning always happens at the right time, when the brain is ready for it.

Part of education is learning about rational reasoning, and Home Education is no exception. One day when he was about 12 years old Simon was with my father and a few of my father's friends. One of them brought up the subject of the Panama Canal and explained how the sea was higher at one end than the other and that it needed locks to get it level. They all thought this was odd, as one would assume that the seas were at the same height around the world. Simon suggested that perhaps, as the earth rotated, there would be an amount of drag on the water of the seas to produce this inequality. They were all impressed with his observation, which demonstrated an imaginative, visual power of reasoning.

'Nothing that is worth knowing can be taught.'

~ Oscar Wilde

Some children accessed formal learning, GCSEs and other examinations when they were old enough to attend the local Further Education college and some chose to enrol in Open University courses and study at home. Many of them then went on to Higher Education at university.

Social Awareness

Something that is encouraged in our education system is citizenship. This covers seven different aspects of life: cooperation, which is about working together as a group or team; patience is the quality of being patient and even-tempered; fairness considers the common good as well as individual desires; respect is about accepting your fellow citizens and acceptance of different cultures; strength of character is being able to stand up for what you believe is right; self-improvement is a continual process throughout life of seeking knowledge and increasing awareness; balance; and patriotism: supporting our nation's ideals, but not to the detriment of other nations.

For me, citizenship is about being an active member of society and supporting one's community and country. It is also about developing self-awareness and an empathy for others.

One evening Simon and I visited my friend Ellen's house where we meet Lauraine, who did a reflexology and massage demonstration. She showed us how to do a basic shoulder massage on another person. Simon was intrigued so I asked Lauraine if she did courses in reflexology. She very kindly offered to organise a one-day course just for Simon and me. This was very enlightening and interesting, and we practised it for a short while afterwards. It gave a greater insight into our personal self-awareness.

Three of the families hosted foreign teenagers for extended periods of time and the corresponding child returned to their homes with them. Some of these exchanges were for up to six months. These children joined in with our Home Education group and improved their English, and, when our children went to their homes, they benefited from the foreign languages and cultures. This was a good cultural exchange.

One day Simon was watching Blue Peter on TV. Their appeal that year was to take bags of clothes to the Blue Cross charity shop, to help raise money to fund the return of African children who had been separated from their families and taken many miles away. Each bag full of clothes added to the total collected. A hundred bags would fund one child to be returned home, so Simon's target was to help return one child.

We collected bags of clothes from the families of the Home Education group and from our friends and family.

Eventually Simon achieved his aim and received a Blue Peter badge for his efforts.

James became a St John's Ambulance cadet. This offers a great opportunity for young people to get involved with volunteering, learning first aid and building confidence and leadership skills.

These diverse and varied activities demonstrate how these unique individuals have grown into responsible, caring adults who are functioning members of society.

ROBOTICS Team (FLL)

When Shena first bought James a Lego Mindstorm kit she did some research online and found the First Lego League International Competition, which was a worldwide tournament based on this kit. She also found that there was a regional competition held in Swindon, so we all went along to watch it. Afterwards the children all felt they could do better than the school teams we had watched. So, the following year, Shena entered our team of 11 children and we duly received the competition topic, notes, challenge mat and challenges, made from Lego, that needed assembling. The competition consisted of four sections: robot design including a presentation, robot performance, a research project including a presentation, and teamwork.

The robot design is based on the different challenges to be performed on the mat. This involves building the robot to our team's design and then accessing the computer to programme it to do the necessary actions. The team are also expected to present the robot to the judges and explain how it works. Throughout the competition they are observed and marked on their teamwork.

The challenge mat was a fixed size and standard layout for everyone around the world and there is a 'knock out' element on the challenge mat, commonly referred to as 'on the table'. This is where two teams have two minutes to complete the most actions and attract the most points, until there is an overall winner.

Each year the competition is based on a different theme and our first year was Ocean Odyssey. The project the team chose was 'The Effect of Noise Pollution in the Oceans on Whales and Dolphins'. As part of this research we arranged a visit to the Whale and Dolphin Conservation Centre in Chippenham, where they presented a special talk just for us. The team came home with posters and literature about whales and dolphins, including information on the noise pollution problem. This was quite an eye opener for all of us. Sonar travels a very long way through water and as these marine mammals, or Cetacea, communicate by sound, any alien sounds detrimentally disrupt their orientation, movement and communication.

Coincidentally, on the morning of the national competition in Loughborough, the news headline was about a young whale that was stuck in the River Thames in London. Needless to say, this was incorporated in their presentation!

There were three levels to the competition – the regionals, the nationals and the internationals. The first two were held in each competing country and the winners of each country qualified to go to the top international competition held in the US. The other qualifying teams were invited to compete at an alternative international competition. Our team went to the Open European Championship in Eindhoven in Holland the first year; the second year was held in Scandinavia, but unfortunately the eruption of the Icelandic volcano seriously restricted teams being able to get there; the third year our team went to the Open Asian Championship in Tokyo, Japan.

Shena, Heidi and the team demonstrated this at HESFES one year and there are now other home educated teams successfully competing, one of which actually went to the US championship a few years later.

Lego Mindstorm kits are used in schools and universities around the world. The simple use of the Lego and the basic computer programme is brilliant for getting children interested in the science of robotics. They are also used as an introduction in different university courses including engineering, design, robotics and computing.

~~~

Each family brought something different to the group commensurate with their own interests and skills, and this provided us with so many interesting and diverse activities that this list here is not exhaustive. Learning does not necessarily only happen in a classroom or in school, though sadly this is often the belief. Shena once told me about a time when the daughter of her friend joined them for dinner after she had come home from school. Over the dinner table Shena started a conversation about something they had been doing during the day. When Shena tried to include her friend's daughter in the conversation the prompt reply was "That is school work and I don't do school work outside of school!"

I believe that every opportunity is a learning opportunity. Learning can and does take place 24/7/365 anywhere, everywhere and at any time – and we didn't get it wrong.

'There are many problems, but I think there is a solution to all these problems; it's just one, and it's education.'

~ Malala Yousafzai

'If a seed of a lettuce will not grow, we do not blame the lettuce. Instead the fault lies with us for not having nourished the seed properly.'

~ Buddhist proverb

Chapter 7
Exploration of Home Education

Why Home Education?

When Simon was struggling at school and the system was failing him, I was desperate. I had a child who was becoming increasingly miserable, introverted and stressed, so I began to research the alternatives, which seemed to be:

- Keep him in the state system
- Steiner Wardorf schools
- Private school system
- Home schooling
- Home Education

When I discussed Simon's problems with the headmistress, she suggested that I could try a different school and, though this may have solved the immediate issue of bullying and Simon's relationship with his class teacher, I realised we could have the same issues again, as he was also having problems was his school work and keeping up with his peers, so I decided against it.

I had come across some of Rudolf Steiner's philosophy and his child development concepts, which made sense to me, so I decided to investigate the Steiner Wardorf Schools that were based on his teachings.

The first thing I did was to send an email to the head office of the Steiner Wardorf Schools Fellowship asking about their schools and suggesting that I was considering Home Education. Sadly, their reply advised me that Home Education should be my last resort – but they offered me little encouragement for anything else.

I researched different Steiner Wardorf Schools, where they were, what age range they catered for, whether they were residential or daily attendance. One that sounded quite good was in south Devon, which was too far away, but one near Stroud was having an open day. The school was about a 60-mile round trip and I would have been prepared to do it twice a day if this school proved suitable for Simon, so I went along to visit.

However, as we were shown around the school, I did not feel that it really reflected Rudolf Steiner's philosophy of child learning and development. We were shown classrooms with rows of desks and children sitting facing the blackboard. I found out that most of their style of teaching was didactic, which would not have suited Simon. While visiting this school I went into their small book shop where I found a very useful book, *Free Range Education: How Home Education Works* by Terri Dowty. I cried on the way home from this Steiner School as I felt it was not significantly different from the state school system. Thankfully, when I read the book I had bought, I found it was inspiring and helped me to have the courage to seriously consider Home Education.

I discussed a private school with a parent whose children attended one near Cirencester. Though the cost would have caused a level of hardship, this school system didn't appeal to me. It was a very long day, as they travelled by coach morning and evening, and it included Saturday mornings. I looked at their son, who was the same age as Simon: he looked very tired, with bags under his eyes, and he had become withdrawn. My instincts told me that this school would likely present the same problems we already had with Simon.

The daughter of a customer of mine attended a private home for her education. The family ran this facility for their own children and brought in private tutors; they allowed a small number of children to join them at a nominal cost. This was "Home Schooling" in the true sense. In March 2002 Simon and I watched a Channel 4 documentary about different methods of educating children away from school. It featured the "Home School" and my customer's daughter.

I chose Home Education because of the bullying and the school system, which was not working for Simon. He was clearly becoming withdrawn and bottling his frustrations. Having taken the decision to remove Simon from school we became part of an active Home Education group based in Swindon and we are all still friends now. We all followed our own form of child-centred autonomous learning, and joined in with lots of group activities.

'What we want to see is the child in pursuit of knowledge, not knowledge in pursuit of the child.'

~ George Bernard Shaw

What is Home Education?

For me the difference between 'Home Schooling' and 'Home Education' is that the first is a school in someone's own home. The dictionary definition of home schooled is "...at home being taught by the parents" whereas Home Education is about not going to a formal school or institution. However, the term 'Home Education' still implies being taught at home, which is actually very far from what we did – as you will have seen in Chapter 6!

When I was asked about Simon's education, I would say that we followed a 'child-centred autonomous learning' process, which literally meant that if Simon showed an interest in something, we pursued it and if he didn't, we didn't. Today this is known as 'unschooling'. Taking this unschooling philosophy to the wider picture of life is known as radical unschooling, or whole life unschooling, and is applied to every area of a child's life, not just education, though you could argue that all life is about learning and having the freedom to learn. This is certainly the path we took alongside the other families in this book.

There are many ways to facilitate the learning or education of children other than in the formal regime of a school classroom, though society has quite a rigid, deep-rooted belief of what education and learning is, formed over generations. Perhaps it is time to question the deeply embedded metaphors on how we relate to the reality around us.

Is Home Education legal?

At the time that Simon was refusing to go to school and subsequently announced that he didn't want to go to school any more, I was more concerned about his emotional wellbeing than if I was breaking the law, even though I am, and always have been, law abiding.

If you pose the question "Who is responsible for children's education?" most people will say that the responsibility lies with "the school" and they would be rather surprised to find out to the contrary. The headmistress told me that it was the law for Simon to attend school, but I knew that I could take lawful responsibility for his education. In fact, in the first instance it is the parent or carer's responsibility to decide on their children's educational path.

The Law

Section 7 of the 1996 Education Act states that it is the duty of parents to secure education for children of compulsory school age.

"The parent of every child of compulsory school age shall cause him to receive efficient full-time education suitable:

a) to his age, ability and aptitude, and

b) to any special educational needs he may have,

either by regular attendance at school or otherwise."

"...at school

or otherwise"

As a parent, you must make sure your child receives a full-time education from the age of five, but you don't have to follow the national curriculum and it doesn't necessarily need to be at school. It is the education that is compulsory – not the school.

Home Education comes under the 'or otherwise' part of the law and that is where Education Otherwise got their name.

The local authority can make an 'informal enquiry' to check your child is getting a suitable education at home; however, they do not have any authority unless they suspect that the parent is not fulfilling their parental obligation. In this case the authority needs to legally prove it before they are able to serve a school attendance order.

When Simon refused go to school, I was advised by IPSEA (Independent Panel for Special Education Advice) to contact the Education Welfare Officer (EWO) before they came knocking on my door, as Simon was still legally registered at the school. This was when I first met Mr Rigby, who was very helpful and supportive, and he advised me to send a letter of de-registration to the school.

From the beginning of home educating Simon I kept a photographic and video record of all our activities. This was to ensure that I could prove he was participating in a wide range of activities.

Education Otherwise, which is a national organisation for home educators, produce a card for home educated children to carry. It quotes the law on one side and has an explanation that the child is legitimately out of school on the other. Simon carried one of these and he regrets that he was never stopped by a truancy officer. Both James and Dan were stopped, at different times. Dan was stopped one day by a community police officer when he was walking the five minutes to James's house! James was in Swindon town one day with his mum, Shena, and they had separated to do their own shopping. James had a present for Shena hidden inside his coat, as he didn't want her to see it. He was stopped by a truancy officer, who asked what he had inside his coat and wanted to take him to the police station, even though he showed her his Education Otherwise card. Thankfully Shena came along at that moment and backed up James's story.

At our Home Education group, Shena was our 'go to' person with regards to the law and dealing with the authorities. She was able to quote the law and she was also the local representative for Education Otherwise.

The pros and the cons of Home Education

When I spoke to the families featured in this book, I asked each of the children what they liked and disliked about being home educated. Here are their answers.

Likes

Freedom was the most common answer – freedom to choose what they did and when they wanted to do it. Freedom to access the sports facilities when they were almost empty, and freedom to take holidays at any time without consequence of higher costs or fines.

Simon ~ *"Being home educated was the best time of my life to date. I had the freedom to do what I wanted and when I wanted to."*

Ruby ~ *"For me, the best thing about being home educated was having freedom."*

James ~ *"I was quite happy being educated from home."*

Colin ~ *"I had the freedom to do what I wanted and I was still learning in the process."*

Aidan ~ *"I enjoyed the freedom to be able to pursue what I was interested in."*

Dan ~ *"I felt free, safe and happy."*

Dislikes

The main dislike was the general feeling of disapproval from members of society who believed that children should go to school.

There was some feeling of not having an appreciation of time management and timetabling, and the lack of repetitive practice did not help when they subsequently joined mainstream further education.

Simon ~ *"In the very beginning I felt embarrassed and self-conscious when going out when there were no other children about."*

Ruby ~ *"I didn't like it when some adults would quiz me."*

James ~ *"I felt a bit frustrated when I was asked by adults what year I was in."*

Colin ~ *"Doing my first degree through Open University at home, I realised that I missed the university experience."*

Aidan ~ *"I found that I was not as quick as I needed to be when given a time constraint."*

Dan ~ *"I went to college to meet more people."*

De-schooling

De-schooling is about unlearning what was learnt at school. The emotional trauma; the feeling of inadequacy; bottling the anguish; being crushed under the weight of the education system; feeling sick every morning waiting for the bus; depression. This list is not exhaustive, but it does describe where Simon was when he took his first step away from this institution.

The biggest sadness for me was that he had become too scared to try anything in case he got it wrong. This took him a long time to move on from, and it still very occasionally rears its ugly head sometimes, over 17 years later.

To facilitate de-schooling, it is necessary to give your child the space to just be. To explore who they are and what they are interested in. No pressure or expectations, no need for them to think about the school stuff, which caused them pain.

'There is no end to education. It is not that you read a book, pass an examination, and finish with education.
The whole of life, from the moment you are born to the moment you die,
is a process of learning.'

~ Jiddu Krishnamurti

'Expecting all children the same age to learn from the same materials is like expecting all children the same age to wear the same size clothing.'

~ Madeline Hunter

Chapter 8
Frequently Asked Questions

This chapter covers the questions we were most often asked about the lives of our children, as they were outside of social conventions. However, I believe what people really wanted to ask was how does it work? How will my child fit in or learn anything? Can I manage to organise our lives when the children are with me all the time?

Though we said we were home educating, in reality the learning or education was not compartmentalised from our day to day life. I look at the bigger picture of what is best for my child and how we can make it work.

How do the children socialise?

This is the main concern of most people when we talk about Home Education, as most people assume that the children are literally being 'schooled' at home in isolation. Society's belief is that children can only socialise at school. This really is not true, especially if a child is shy or being bullied. In fact, the school regime does not reflect the social strata of the outside world.

At school they are clumped together with their own age group and often their own gender. How is this representative of society at large?

If you have no friends or common interests in a crowd then this is not socialising.

I found three main meanings of the verb 'to socialise':

- (Go Out) ...to spend time, when you are not working, with friends or other people in order to enjoy yourself.
- (Train) To train people or animals to behave in a way that others in the group think is suitable.
- To spend time with other people for pleasure.

In my opinion, none of these describe time spent at school. At school children are expected to sit quietly and get on with their work without talking. So school is about working and not necessarily enjoying yourself with friends. Maybe school is a place where training happens, but this is still not what society means by socialising at school. The current school system is designed to mould children to conform to a narrow set of rules, which makes them reactive to orders and discourages their self-willed proactivity. The school system is not set up for spending time with other people for pleasure.

*'It is better to be alone
than in bad company.'*

~ George Washington

So why does society at large think that school is the only place for children to be able to socialise?

I was asked what my aim was in home educating Simon. I was aware of the statistics that 80% of children who truanted were boys; that there was and still is a growing incidence of suicide in teenage boys and young men; increasing depression in young teenagers. Clearly the school system was failing boys and I didn't want Simon to be one of those statistics. It is not only boys who are being failed by this system; however, as I had a son my focus was predominately on the statistics about boys.

My reply to this question was that I wanted to produce a well-rounded, functional, happy adult. I would only see the proof of this years later. In fact, now Simon is 27 years old he is all that I had hoped for.

This well-rounded adult was clearly not going to happen by going to school and I had the tools in my hands to do something about it.

Simon had been so traumatised at school he was worried about being in large groups who might bully him so when he went to trampoline lessons at the local sports centre or other activities I would need to stay with him for him to feel safe. This was also the situation when he was walking along the high street: if there was a crowd or even a few young lads, Simon would cross the road or go the other way rather than pass them. Being at school had made him feel nervous about being sociable with strangers.

What is Socialising?

Our Home Education group met at a church hall in Swindon. There were about 25 families who met regularly, and maybe 6 or 7 families at a time at this regular weekly meeting. At these meetings each family would bring along some sort of activity – box games, craft materials, other toys – and on special occasions we might have parties or quizzes. We, the adults, often drank coffee, ate cake and chatted, while the children would interact and do whatever they wanted to. There would typically be toddlers to teenagers, boys and girls all mixing together and also including the adults.

On the same day as one of these group meetings Simon and I went to the local village firework display in the evening, where Simon met up with some boys who he had been to school with. I looked across the recreation field and saw six distinct groups of children amongst the adults. There were boys separate from the girls; there were toddlers, youngsters and teenagers all in separate groups … and none of these groups were interacting. This was starkly in contrast to the afternoon group activity. These were school groups!

Our group met up as families, which gave us a strength of unity, and we all felt a level of responsibility towards members of the other families. We still have a strong link to some of the parents and grown-up children now, 17 years later.

So socialising actually happens better outside of the school environment. It is about mixing with people of similar interests, regardless of age and gender, and enjoying the company of friends and family in different situations. Helping and supporting each other.

More recently, Simon, Colin and Aidan have set up a board gaming group in our local village hall where they meet twice a month. This is for anyone of any age who wants play board games. There are even young children who join in with their parents. They have a Facebook group and it is advertised in the local parish magazines. Simon gets funding so they can offer this activity for free. This is about socialising and actively being part of the community.

I think it is important to encourage children to learn to rely on their own intuition to assess people. This makes them stronger and helps them to make appropriate decisions for themselves, which would also help to keep them safe.

How do you balance life, work, children, family and learning?

Having a child with you 24/7 does not necessarily mean that it is difficult to work or earn a living. I took Simon with me to my workplace where he was able to help with the horses or use the computer. Shena worked from home and completed most of her work early in the morning. Jane was able to take her children to craft fairs and markets with her. Mandy and Heidi were supported by their husbands. Some couples share the task so they can divide their time between being responsible for the children and following their own work.

Sometimes it is possible to share the care of each other's children in the group, or family members may help. This enables you to have some personal time separate from the children.

How do children fit into our society?

The 'us and them' divide that is evident in the classroom, at school, between the adults and the children, causes a massive chasm and children become invisible. 'Children should be seen and not heard' is a classic belief left over from the Victorian era.

Society has evolved in a way that does not respect children or give them a voice and I believe this is why children often do not feel they can talk to their parents or an adult, because they are not given a right to express their views, either by society or other adults. Our society ostracises children from socialising with the wide spectrum of society and adults often socialise without their children, and then, when they get to 18, they are expected to be functioning adults when they have not had any experience of how to behave other than at school, in an institution where they are grouped with their age peers and often their own gender. Society wonders why we have disaffected teenagers, increasing incident of suicides and depression in our youth and fatal knife crimes. So sad.

I was disgusted a few years ago when a group of us – six adults and three young teenagers, including Simon – visited Oxford. We went to about six different places to have lunch and none of them would allow the children in with us. We eventually ended up in a Pizza Hut.

Over the years of being a riding instructor I began to

realise that adults talk over the top of children and often do not introduce them. I began to acknowledge the children by asking their name or addressing my questions to them. Sometimes I could see the surprise on their faces, as if suddenly they were no longer invisible, and sometimes they would not respond because they had not realised I was actually addressing them.

My view, as a parent, is that Simon was my responsibility from the beginning. I do not agree with dumping young babies with a child minder or a nursery for long periods of time. This must be harmful to their emotional development. When Simon was at school, I began to consider whether I would choose that teacher to have an influence on him. If the answer was no, then why was I letting him be in her class?

As a parent I had an expectation of a certain level of behaviour from Simon, not only when we were out in company, but at all times. When Simon was about 11 we watched an item of news about adults or parents not hitting or smacking their children. Simon said he thought that adults should not hit children for any reason and I said there needed to be a meeting point halfway in a child's behaviour. We discussed what each of us expected from our relationship and we have been able to be open about all subjects. I believe Simon has always behaved as a functional member of society. If you expect your child to misbehave or be a nuisance then you are setting them up to fail. Your reticular filter is set to see the misbehaviour and not the good things.

Children are part of society, part of our family and our lives. To be functioning members of society they need to be integrated in all aspects of life and society within the protection of their parents or responsible adults. Pushing them out of the family environment at a very young age can only be stressful for them. I believe that radical unschooling is the best way to raise emotionally balanced adults.

What constitutes 'full time education'?

We imagine that a full-time education, being a replication of school, is from 9am in the morning to 3pm in the afternoon, five days each week. This is a full-time job. How does this fit into family life? But in reality a child at school would not be learning for this length of time and would certainly not have that much teacher time. In fact, if you look at the amount of time at school spread over 365 days rather than the weekdays of three terms it is just over two hours each day. And then if you take into consideration that a child at school is one of many then the teacher time pro rata works out as little over five minutes each day! Also, when you see that learning just happens, at any time and any place, it is easy to realise that a child being home educated will learn while the family just gets on with living their life.

Here is the maths relating to full time education.

If you consider that a child is at school from 9am to 3pm 35 weeks each year:

5 hours x 5 days x 35 weeks = 875 hours per year maximum. That does not take into account the school outings, assemblies, school sports day, teacher training days, etc.

If that learning was spread over 365 days, then 875 hours / 365 days = 2½ hours per day.

If the class has approximately 25 children, each child would have an average of 12 minutes one to one teacher time each day. If there is one child requiring more time, then another child loses out.

12 minutes x 5 days x 35 weeks = 35 hours/ year

35 hours / 365 days = 5.75 minutes per day.

[At Further Education colleges, full time is about 16 hours a week, 30 weeks per year.

16 hours X 30 weeks = 480 hours per year

480 hours / 365 days = approx. 1.5 hours/day]

As I said earlier, I believe every opportunity is a learning opportunity, so learning can and does take place even when you are going about your daily routine of shopping or cooking, doing general household chores or looking after the animals. Children absorb what they are interested in, so, during the 24 hours of a day there will be more than 2.5 hours of learning and certainly more than 12 minutes 1 to 1 interaction! In fact, 'full time' can fit around your life and daily routine.

When Simon was about 12 years old, I started going to a monthly meeting in Bristol called Yes Group, Bristol! and he would come with me and mix with the otherwise adult group. He was always interested and involved in whatever the meeting was about and who the speaker was, and he was absorbing the culture and diversity of the group.

When we bought our alpaca we started attending some spinning, weaving and dying guilds. Simon enjoyed joining in with these groups and became a functioning member amongst the more elderly members, as he would help move tables and chairs; he joined the weaving group and also learnt how to knit, amongst other craft activities. We also joined the Westbury Woollies, a knitting machine group, and we went along to a braiding group in Aldbourne. My mother would join us, as she was an avid crafter.

Simon's father worked and lived abroad most of the time, so he had very little input into how we pursued our Home Education life.

What costs are involved with having your child with you 24/7?

Home educating your child or children does not necessarily have to be expensive. In fact, there are some significant savings. No school uniform or sports equipment; no school trips; you can take holidays whenever you want, and you don't have to go at the most expensive times.

We were fortunate that Simon's father earnt a good salary and was able to support our activities, even though he was rarely with us.

I was running a riding centre when Simon first came out of school and Simon would come with me, and he was able to pursue the activities he was interested in. He was allowed to use the computer there and helped with our horses and ponies.

We had a very active group of families, each of whom brought their own interests to the group. Some activities that were organised cost nothing. Walking on the Wiltshire Downs, having picnics, meeting at Lydiard Park or Queen's Garden cost us nothing. Bowood House had an annual pass, which made each weekly session quite cheap. Joining in organised activities like trampolining or drama did attract a cost; however, we were discerning in choosing what activities Simon wanted to do. Group meetings had a nominal fee to cover the cost of the hall. Swindon Council had membership cards to their sports facilities, which gave reduced price access to the swimming pool and ice rink. Swindon Young Musicians, which met on Saturday mornings, was reasonably priced. I trawled the charity shops for box games, fun books and other items of potential interest. As a group, we shared ideas, activities and learning materials and now there is so much online that makes it so much easier to research interests.

Tutors

Most of us didn't employ tutors for specialist subjects. We were accessing a lot of activities and the learning was incidental.

When the Robotics team for the First Lego League International (FLL) competitions started the focus on their competition entry was paramount. This took up a lot of their time and totally absorbed them, and we raised funds from sponsorships, donations and by running courses in Robotics to help reduce our individual costs for entering and travelling to the competitions.

Both Simon and James signed up for the Electronic Wizard Wonder Boxes, which they received fortnightly over 20 weeks. They also attended some electronic workshops, which attracted a cost.

So it is possible to work around the needs of the children, by finding relatively inexpensive activities and sharing knowledge and resources.

The cost of exams

Some parents self-funded the Open University courses that their children took.

At 16 years of age, home educated children were able to access the local Further Education college in Swindon, New College. By attending full time they were able to attract funding for their courses and examinations. Dan went to New College at the age of 14 for one year and his parents were obliged to pay for his courses and examinations until he was 16 years old.

'If you think education is expensive, try ignorance.'

~ Andy McIntyre

Financial education

As one of Simon's activities I opened a bank account for him, at the Halifax, which came with a debit card. I worked out how much all the activities cost and set up a monthly standing order to his account to cover these costs. He was then responsible for ensuring he had enough money on him, and he paid for all his activities. By doing this, he learned to understand the value of money and how to use it, as, when he was younger, he had no comprehension or feeling of responsibility of the value of money.

As we would access free or low-cost activities, it was possible to structure the family life, earning and facilitating the children's education in a balanced way.

Do you need to be a teacher?

This question really refers to a number of different considerations: the legality of home educating, am I clever enough, do I need to be qualified, how can I teach my child everything?

"How do I take over responsibility for my child's education without becoming that dreaded 'teacher'?"

I did not formally teach Simon; I facilitated his learning and we followed his interests. If that meant he did not read a book or write something, that was fine. It was probably about two years before he picked up a pencil. This was his period of de-schooling.

How do you teach the different subjects?

It is not necessary for the parent to know everything (or anything!) about various subjects, and each subject does not need to happen in isolation of all other subjects. There is enough information out there to help further children's interests. It *is* necessary, however, to appreciate the commitment and fun of Home Education.

'We discovered that education is not something which the teacher does, but that it is a natural process which develops spontaneously in the human being.'

~ Maria Montessori

How do children learn?

It is generally believed that the only way to learn is at school or in some sort of institution, so when I first took Simon out of school his father phoned me from abroad, where he was working. "I am concerned that if Simon doesn't go to school, he won't get any qualifications," he said. I replied that I thought if he *did* go to school, he wouldn't get any qualifications.

Because Simon's school experience had taught him that learning hurt, and he couldn't see the point to reading and found writing difficult, I decided to use a chart of Gardner's eight intelligences to demonstrate that learning could be a positive experience. (See Chapter 9.)

Simon soon realised that learning took place all the time and he began to see the benefits of reading by using his computer regularly.

The following four stories demonstrate how learning takes place while doing something else.

1. Pulling Ragwort

I have a field for my horses and it is necessary to remove the ragwort, as it is a poisonous plant. The best way to remove it is to dig it up, roots and all, and put it in a plastic bag. It is important to wear gloves while handling it. While Simon and I were dealing with the ragwort we were discussing it being poisonous and talking about why it was poisonous. There is a caterpillar who gets its poison from this plant. We then went on to talk about the need for plants and the tropical rain forests for the absorption of carbon dioxide; the oxygen/carbon dioxide exchange in plants. I also described the molecular structure and the combining powers of oxygen and carbon.

This was all while we were digging up ragwort.

2. Counting Bales

The horses had ad lib hay provided for them in two circular hay feeders. Simon and I would collect 40 bales in the trailer and then unload them directly into the feeders. As we were unloading the hay, I would ask him how many bales would be in each feeder – forty divided by two equals twenty. We knew the horses usually ate about three bales per day, so how many days would these last? Forty divided by three equals thirteen with one remaining, so if today is Tuesday, when will we need to buy some more? Two weeks Monday.

… and we were still unloading hay bales.

3. WW1 Foot Rot

One day, as we were going somewhere in the car, I was explaining to Simon about the condition in horses' feet called thrush, which is caused by them standing in wet conditions continuously. I then brought up the subject of the WW1 trench warfare. Simon proceeded to tell me about how the soldiers got foot rot when they were in the trenches. I was rather surprised and asked him where he had learnt that. "On the telly!" was his reply.

4. Transit of Venus

In 1999 we had travelled to northern France to witness the full solar eclipse of the sun by the moon. It was amazing how the farm animals all cushed, laid down, as the false, apparent dusk materialised. We used Simon's binoculars to reflect the image of the moon onto a plain surface, as it is dangerous to actually look at the sun even when it is eclipsed by the moon. When Venus transited the sun in 2004, we had been invited to visit the observatory near Marlborough but, unfortunately, we were unable to join the group for this activity, so Simon got out his binoculars and a piece of white paper and repeated what we had done with the solar eclipse. Venus, being much closer to the sun, appeared as a tiny dot in comparison to the moon, which covered most of the sun.

How do children who are outside of the education system access exams and gain qualifications?

How home educated children take examinations and gain qualifications is a common concern for people who are not part of the Home Education community. GCSEs at 16 and on to A Levels is not the only route; in fact, it is a very restrictive and somewhat blinkered way to achieve qualifications. Throughout our home educating time Simon achieved several qualifications in trampolining, Association of British Riding Schools certificates in riding and horse care, and cycling proficiency, amongst other things. Simon went on to study subjects he was interested in at college.

Other members of our group went along different paths. Colin attained piano and drama qualifications; Lamda gold medal in public speaking; British Horse Society (BHS) Horse Owner's Certificate level 1; as well as doing Open University courses from the age of 14. Aidan also took the BHS certificate, Open University courses and is about to complete his first degree. Both James and his sibling took Open University courses from their early teens. James also pursued his music.

Dan went to New College to take some GCSEs. Ruby learned many life skills and she learned how to think and seek out information for herself. Many subjects were covered this way and she developed a fairly well-rounded understanding of most subjects.

These examples demonstrate that learning is fluid and knowledge is transferable. No subject is studied in isolation of any other. Learning can happen theoretically or through practical experience. It is about giving children the freedom to learn what they want to learn or are interested in: to follow their journey and do it wherever and whenever they choose.

Having said that children learn organically, it is accepted that formal qualifications are necessary to pursue a career, especially if they choose to follow a profession as a teacher, doctor, solicitor, etc. However, 16 is not the only age to be able to take GCSE examinations, and GCSEs are not the only route to further or higher education. Colin, who is currently studying for his PhD, did not take any GCSEs but studied Open University courses at home throughout his teenage years.

'Intellectual growth should commence at birth and cease only at death.'

~ Albert Einstein

'Many of life's failures are people who did not realise how close they were to success when they gave up.'

~ Thomas A. Edison

Chapter 9
Learning Styles and
Personality Profiles

Having taught riding, run evening classes and trained horses and other animals I have become aware that everyone learns differently, at different times and at different rates.

There are a number of educationalists and philosophers who expound their theories on child development and learning, but one of my favourite child behaviourists is actually a horse trainer.

Monty Roberts was the original horse whisperer and besides training wild horses he also fostered many troubled children.

Monty said: "I am not for a moment suggesting that animals and humans are the same but, psychologically speaking, their behavioural patterns have more similarities than they have differences.

"Horses and children are almost identical emotionally and psychologically: they are both flight animals who wish to avoid trouble, but will become first bashful, then aggressive, if intimidated."

According to Monty Roberts, the main fault with education systems is that they expect a high level of achievement in children, then punish them for not succeeding.

I have found this to be true with horses and children alike. Without being given adequate information or help, the failure of the horse to perform or child to succeed is then criticised or punished. Aggression toward horses is common and children are given negative feedback, which makes them feel unworthy. When a horse fails to do what you wanted him to do then you have not asked the right question. If a child fails to do the task then it hasn't been explained clearly enough or they are not ready to do the task.

Child development

As well as children developing at different rates, they all have their own specific learning styles and needs. For example, when Simon was first learning to speak, he would often transpose consonants, so he would say melon instead of lemon, which became even more confusing when he said lemon for melon! This was amusing and rather cute, but I didn't realise until much later that this is a classic sign of dyslexia. Another indication of dyslexia that I missed was his inability to recite nursery rhymes or remember songs.

From almost the moment Simon started walking I recognised he was very right-handed and -footed and I used this to my advantage when crossing the road. I would say: "Toes," which meant toes on the curb; "look both ways, all clear; left foot, go!" This would stop him briefly to think which foot to move first, as his automatic instinct would be his right foot and this prevented him rushing out into the road.

Early on, Simon showed no interest in colouring or painting or holding any sort of drawing or writing tool. When given a pencil he would hold it like a dagger and when he started school he found it difficult to wield a pencil. He would lean his hand heavily on the table and struggle to make any mark on the paper. At this stage he still needed to develop his hand/eye coordination, which was evident after I had taken him to an Educational Kinesiologist when he couldn't ride a 2-wheeler bicycle. By Year 3 he was still not forming his letters very well because of his way of holding the pencil so tightly, which made it almost impossible for him to do cursive writing.

When Simon went to college they assessed him for dyslexia and on a scale of 0–4 Simon was a 2.4. However, his biggest issue was short term memory. When he looked at the board, by the time he turned to his book he had forgotten what he had seen, which probably ties in with his inability to remember songs and nursery rhymes. At the other end of the scale he scored 100% on a task that was about recognising the pattern of a sequence and identify the following one.

Because children all have different needs when it comes to learning, it's important to be aware of the tools available to decipher their preferred learning style. There are a huge number of tools available but here I am going to take a look at the following systems that I like to use: Educational Kinesiology®, VARK learning styles, Multiple Intelligences, Kolb's Learning Cycle, and DISC profiling.

Educational Kinesiology®

Educational Kinesiology® is based on simple movements that stimulate different communications in the brain.

My sister first introduced me to Edu-K (Educational Kinesiology®), or Brain Gym, because she had experienced significant results using it with her youngest daughter. She subsequently trained as a Brain Gym practitioner and we were lucky enough to be her 'guinea pigs' and experience the positive effects of this process.

The Brain Gym programme includes repeating certain simple movements such as bilateral or cross crawling (a way of simultaneously using both the left and right sides of the brain by touching your left knee to your right hand, then your right knee to your left hand), yawning, making symbols in the air with arms and hands, and doodling with one or the other hand – or both together. It also advocates drinking enough water to ensure sufficient hydration. This is all intended to integrate and help re-pattern brain connections and increase blood flow to the brain. The organisation claims the methods are grounded in good neuroscience, which deals with the function of the nervous system and the brain.

One of the underlying ideas is that the exercises are meant to 'balance' the brain hemispheres so the two sides work together better; there is also a notion of integrating the top parts of the brain with the lower parts of the brain to integrate thought and emotion, as well as integrating visual, auditory, and motor skills.

This process uses movement to build pathways in the brain and improve coordination. Edu-K highlights how important it is for babies to experience the whole range of movements, from rolling through crawling to walking at the appropriate time commensurate to their own developmental time scale.

VARK Learning Styles

Learning styles are a popular concept in psychology and education and are intended to identify how people learn best. The VARK model of learning styles suggests that there are four main types of learners. These four key types are:

– Visual (spatial) learners
– Auditory (aural-musical) learners
– Reading/writing (verbal-linguistic) learners
– Kinaesthetic (physical) learners

Simon is a kinaesthetic learner, which means he learns best by engaging his large and small muscle groups by moving around. He cannot just sit still and do the work; he needs to be moving, even in a small way, to be able to listen or access learning. As the school classroom system actively discourages any movement this made it difficult for Simon to access what was going on.

There was one occasion when Simon read a page of a book out loud to me and afterwards said he had no idea what he had just read; the information had not been retained in his mind. This indicates that he is not a reading/writing learner.

More recently Simon has found that he can access audio books best when he is doing physical activities, like gardening. When he stops moving he finds he cannot concentrate on what he is listening to.

'Tell me and I'll forget; show me and I may remember; involve me and I'll understand.'

~ Chinese proverb

- A visual learner prefers to use pictures and images. They have a spatial awareness.
- An aural learner enjoys music and sounds. They learn through listening.
- A verbal learner is good with words and languages, both in speech and writing.
- A kinaesthetic learner needs movement or physical touch to facilitate their learning.

It is useful to have an appreciation of your child's preferred learning style to help facilitate their learning. We all exhibit a preference, though we will have a mixture of all of them.

Sometimes it is evident what a person's preferred learning styles is by how they behave: for example, preferring to listen to something or look at something or touch something. Or what they say; for example, they might say: I see what you are saying. I hear what you are saying. I understand what you are saying. I feel what you are saying.

> *'The ultimate of the 21st century will not be those who cannot read and write, but those who cannot learn, unlearn and relearn.'*
>
> *~ Alvin Toffler*

Howard Gardner's Multiple Intelligences

When Simon didn't feel he was learning anything I used Gardner's model of multiple intelligences to demonstrate that what he was doing each day actually constituted learning in different areas of his multiple intelligences. I used a wheel diagram and labelled each of the eight sections with one of the different intelligences.

A. Linguistic-verbal intelligence is any activity that involves words and language. (Word smart)

Reading; writing; talking; languages; listening to words.

B. Mathematical-logical intelligence is any activity that involves numbers and mathematical processes. (Number/reasoning smart)

Using abstract and symbolic thoughts; sequential reasoning; perceive relationships and connections.

C. Visual-spatial intelligence involves being able to think in three dimensions and visualise pictures and colours. (Picture smart)

Graphic and artistic skills; active imagination.

D. Bodily-kinaesthetic intelligence is being able to use movement and physical activity. (Body smart)

Good sense of timing; perfection of skills; sports.

E. Musical intelligence is the capacity to discern pitch, timbre, rhythm and tone. (Sound smart)

Aware of sounds; able to replicate and create music.

F. Naturalist intelligence is being sensitive to the natural world and living things. (Nature smart)

Animal carers; botanists; farmers.

G. Interpersonal intelligence is effectively interacting and understanding others. (People smart)

Sensitive to moods and temperaments of others.

H. Intra-personal intelligence is about self-awareness of one's thoughts and feelings. (Self-smart)

Able to plan the direction of their lives; self-motivated.

Since I used this to help Simon recognise his different activities and intelligences another intelligence has been identified:

I. Existential intelligence is about tackling the questions of why we live and why we die. (Life smart)

Sensitivity and capacity to tackle deep questions about human existence.

Learning more about the multiple intelligences can help you to better understand your child's strengths and access a broader range of activities to enable improved learning for your child.

When I first came across Gardner's eight intelligences, I was teaching an evening class at the local college in 'Understanding Horses'. I started to write all my lesson plans to incorporate something that would access each of these intelligences. My biggest struggle was musical, as this is *my* weakest intelligence, so I took along classical music and played it softly in the background. To my surprise the pass mark of my students significantly improved once I changed the format of my lessons.

Kolb's Learning Cycle

Kolb's Learning Cycle demonstrates the interaction with the four stages of experiencing learning. These four processes, followed in order, are necessary for learning to take place.

1. Concrete experience (feeling).

An activist learns through actively experiencing something.

2. Reflective observation (watching).

A reflector thinks about the experience and reflects on their observation before making a judgement.

3. Abstract conceptualisation (thinking).

A theorist researches the meaning of the experience.

4. Active experimentation (doing).

A pragmatist brings research and activity together and makes a plan.

Activist
Experiencing doing
something

Pragmatist
Work on the plan

Reflector
Thinking about what you did

Theorist
Research a concept or
idea

The learner may enter this cycle at any point depending on the situation or environment and will be able to maximise their learning if they proceed through all four processes.

Here is an example of Kolb's Learning Cycle when learning to ride a bicycle:

1. Reflective observation – Thinking about riding and watching another person ride a bike.

2. Abstract conceptualisation – Understanding the theory and having a clear grasp of the biking concept.

3. Concrete experience – Receiving practical tips and techniques from a biking expert.

4. Active experimentation – Leaping on the bike and having a go at it.

Being aware of where someone is in the learning cycle will give a clearer idea of how to approach facilitating their learning process.

I first realised that people learn differently when I was giving a friend a riding lesson on Rhidian. Julie is a body and mind therapist and she is able to explain body movement. On this particular occasion she suggested that I got on Rhidian and as she talked me through my body movements, I described how I was riding to her. When she got on Rhidian I was amazed at how much her riding had noticeably improved. "How has that happened?" I asked. Her reply was, "I have just watched you do it." As I am an activist on Kolb's Cycle, I was surprised that she learnt by watching, which I do not do -

I just get on and do it. She was clearly a reflector.

I had never used demonstration in my riding lessons before as it wasn't something that worked for me! I did use it from then on.

DISC Profiling

DISC assessments help us to understand why we behave and react in the ways that we do and how we best interact with other people. The matrix is divided into four sections: Task Orientated, People Orientated, Faster and Slower, which then illustrate four distinct personality and behaviour styles.

Dominance

A person with a **D** style is involved in shaping the environment by overcoming opposition to accomplish results. They are motivated by winning, competition, success and achieving immediate results. They are described as strong willed, determined and self-confident, but may lack concern for others and may show impatience. They value their personal freedom and independence.

Influence

A person with an **I** style is also involved with shaping the environment, but by influencing or persuading people. They are convincing with a warm, magnetic, enthusiastic optimism. They thrive on social recognition, group activities and relationships and fear loss of influence. They enjoy being the centre of attention and popular.

Steadiness

A person with an **S** style likes cooperating with others to carry out tasks. They are motivated by cooperation, being helpful and sincere appreciation. They demonstrate consistent calmness and predictability, though they may be indecisive on occasions and have a tendency to avoid change. They value loyalty and security.

Conscientiousness

A person with a **C** style is a conscientious worker who ensures quality and accuracy. They value opportunities to gain knowledge and produce expert, quality work, though they may be limited by being over critical and fear being wrong. They value quality and accuracy.

	Task orientated	People orientated
Faster Outgoing	**Dominance** The Go-Getters These people are goal and results orientated/ focused.	**Influence** The Promoters These people are fun-loving and positive.
Slower Reserved	**Conscientiousness** The Examiners These people are pragmatic and efficient.	**Steadiness** The Nurturers These people are patient, nice and comforting.

~~~

I have used these five main tools to assess both my and Simon's learning styles and our individual personal development. This has given us better insight into our strengths and weaknesses and how to better communicate with each other.

In my journey through Home Education I became aware of Asperger's syndrome and autism. I also began to have a better understanding of dyslexia, dyspraxia, dyscalculia and dysgraphia. These are all different learning challenges that need more time than the scope of this book to explain, suffice it to know that they all have an influence on our children's ability to learn in different ways.

I believe we all have some level of learning challenges or differences; however, labelling a child or even an adult can be quite restricting. It gives a reason or excuse for not trying or not stretching the boundaries. I believe that being home educated is a much better way for all children to learn and find themselves and their own interests by having the freedom to learn through radical living.

'It will always seem impossible until it's done.'

~ Nelson Mandela

Conclusion

I am proud to have known and still know these young adults who are the next generation. They will help mould society, improve social views of Home Education and Radical Unschooling and help change the outdated education system that exists in schools and institutions today. I feel empowered to have been part of a radical movement along with a group of strong people who stood up for their children.

Talking with each of these young adults I was impressed by their insight into themselves, their depth of self-awareness and well roundedness. They can express themselves clearly and openly. They are the next generation of proactive thinkers and doers.

'The wise old owl sat in the oak,

The more he heard the less he spoke.

The less he spoke the more he heard.

Why aren't we all like that wise old bird.'

'The woman who follows the crowd will usually go no further than the crowd. The woman who walks alone is likely to find herself in places no one has been before.'

~ Albert Einstein

About the Author

Mother ~ Trainer ~ Facilitator ~ Writer ~ Speaker ~ Volunteer ~ Councillor

Susan Walklate has always followed her passions and she demonstrates the strength of character to follow her own beliefs. As a child she was described as single minded, self-willed and wayward, though she was quiet and maybe introverted; these personality traits were certainly developing and influenced by her father.

Susan was determined to have her own pony and worked diligently toward this aim, which became a reality when she was 15 years old. She was totally responsible for his care and keep, and she worked in Woolworths on Saturdays to earn enough to pay for whatever Orinoko needed.

Having trained as a chemistry teacher and subsequently worked in chemistry laboratories for about two years, she once again followed her dream of working with horses and left this well-paid job to work and train, for a pittance, as a riding instructor in a large commercial riding centre in North London.

Continuing to follow her own path she set up Equestrian Services and built up her clientele whilst taking on any available part-time, temporary jobs. At this stage she also ran an evening class at the local college called Understanding Horses, which ran successfully for 18 years.

So, when her son, Simon, was struggling at school and becoming shut down, it was an obvious step to take full responsibility of him, his education and upbringing. It wasn't necessarily the easiest option, but it was certainly the best option for Simon.

This was a massive learning curve for Susan as it enabled her to step back from the tread mill and humdrum of society and be able to be more aware of the metaphors and influences of our society. She soon identified the ingrained beliefs that life rotates around schools and schooling; the erroneous belief that life is all about money and getting more money, which we are forced to believe can only come through pushing children through the pressures of achieving higher and better educational qualifications, rather than giving them true happiness, comfort and self-awareness throughout a carefree childhood. She realised that children learn organically, principally when they are happy, interested and engaged.

With these beliefs, Susan's core values and tenacious passions have resulted in her becoming more proactive in having a positive influence on the local environment and local government. She is a volunteer on the local Parish Council, instigated a neighbourhood plan for the villages and is an active member of a local good neighbour scheme to support villagers staying within the rural environment.

Susan is now determined to tell the true life stories of the children who were successfully home educated and are now fully functioning adults of society.

Susan has also helped Simon to recognise his life path in his promotion of Home Education in a radical way and being an active member of society.

Susan runs workshops and gives talks on a variety of subjects including Home Education; radical life lessons; learning from horses; and understanding animals.

Contact Susan

Email: book@gableendfarm.co.uk

Website: www.gableendfarm.co.uk

                www.radicallife.co.uk

Twitter: @Gable_End_Farm

LinkedIn: Susan Jillian Walklate

Facebook: @Gable.End.Farm

                @Radical.Home.Education

Tel: +44 (0) 7850 482919

'Be passionate about your life,
learn to live without the fear of failing.

Take a chance,
you just might surprise yourself.'

~ Nishan Panwar

Resources

Book

"Free Range Education", edited by Terri Dowty
How home education works

National Organisation

www.educationotherwise.org
Education is compulsory - school is optional

Learning Styles and Personality Profiles

To receive your *free* child-friendly learning styles assessment send your contact details to: book@gableendfarm.co.uk

Courses

Workshops and online courses available at:

www.radicallife.co.uk

Gardening by Simon Thorley Davies

Facebook: @GreenFingers2008

eLearn with Amy

Interactive live online tutoring with face-to-face style video calls, specialising in tutoring home educated children during the daytime.

Amy Claire Rose Smith has a special fondness for helping home-ed kids achieve greatness because she too was home schooled before going to university.

Email: englishwithamy19@outlook.com
Facebook: @eLearn with Amy
Tel: +44 (0) 7496 315793

Acknowledgements

Thank you to everyone who helped make my journey through home educating Simon an enjoyable experience.

To the families who have contributed to this book.

To **Simon Thorley Davies**, for being my inspiration for this book.

To **Jane Jameson**, who has been a good friend from the beginning and grown through the process.

To **Ruby May Patricia Craven**, who has grown into a beautiful, open, friendly young woman.

To **Shena Deuchars**, who was our support. She helped and encouraged us all to continue on our own paths.

To **James La Fleur**, who is a credit to his family and his mother's vision.

To **Heidi De Wet**, who loved her two sons so much and would be so proud of the young men they have become.

To **Tony Putman**, who has shown strength and support throughout his family's journey.

To **Colin Putman**, who has grown into a self-aware, sociable young man.

To **Aidan Putman**, who has grown into himself and his feelings.

To **Mandy Parsons**, whose vision and determination is inspirational. She is a credit to herself.

To **Dan Parsons**, who is still exploring his inner depths. He is so insightful and able to make meaningful connections with many people.

To **Julia Tucknott**, for writing the foreword and helping Simon through his time at college.

To **Lis McDermott** of Lis McDermott Photography, for the photographs.

To **Alison Thompson**, The Proof Fairy, who helped me through the process of making this book a reality.

To everyone who read the first draft of this book and gave wonderful feedback to make it even better.

Last, but not least, I would like to thank **Ellen Watts** for being such a great friend and for helping me through the struggles to get this book completed.

A big thank you to Butterfly House Publishing for making it all possible.

Printed in Poland
by Amazon Fulfillment
Poland Sp. z o.o., Wrocław

50237753R00087